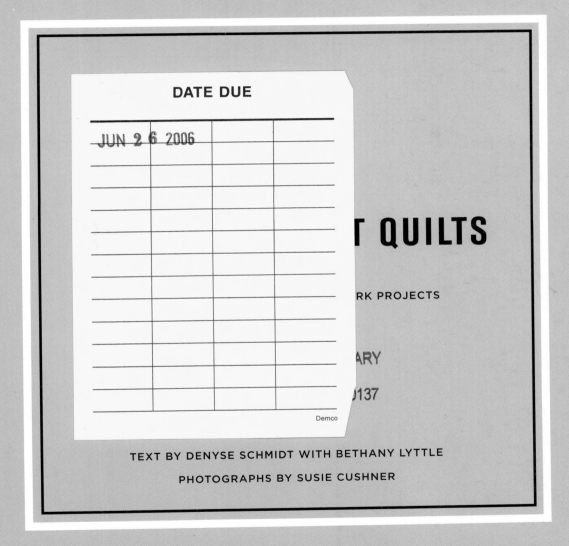

T QUILTS

RK PROJECTS

ARY

0137

TEXT BY DENYSE SCHMIDT WITH BETHANY LYTTLE

PHOTOGRAPHS BY SUSIE CUSHNER

CHRONICLE BOOKS

LIBRARY OF CONGRESS CATALOGING-IN-PUBLICATION DATA:

SCHMIDT, DENYSE. DENYSE SCHMIDT QUILTS : 30 COLORFUL QUILT AND PATCHWORK PROJECTS / TEXT BY DENYSE SCHMIDT WITH BETHANY LYTTLE ; PHOTOGRAPHS BY SUSIE CUSHNER.
P. CM. INCLUDES INDEX.
ISBN 0-8118-4442-0
1. PATCHWORK—PATTERNS.
2. QUILTING—PATTERNS.
I. SCHMIDT, DENYSE.
II. TITLE.
TT835.S3455 2005
746.46'041—DC22
2004023094

DESIGN BY JENNIFER OLSEN, PAPER PLANE STUDIO
STYLING BY JACQUELINE LEMIEUX BOKOR
MANUFACTURED IN CHINA.

DISTRIBUTED IN CANADA BY RAINCOAST BOOKS
9050 SHAUGHNESSY STREET
VANCOUVER, BRITISH COLUMBIA V6P 6E5

10 9 8 7 6 5 4 3 2 1

CHRONICLE BOOKS LLC
85 SECOND STREET
SAN FRANCISCO, CA 94105
WWW.CHRONICLEBOOKS.COM

DENYSE SCHMIDT AND THE PIECES SHE CREATES HAVE ELEVATED THE CRAFT OF QUILTING AND OTHER FABRICATIONS. HER SENSE OF COLOR, STYLE, AND WIT WERE TRULY THE GUIDING LIGHT AND INSPIRATION FOR US IN ILLUSTRATING HER BOOK. I WOULD LIKE TO THANK JACQUELINE BOKOR FOR BRINGING HER TALENT AND HER COMMITMENT TO THE PROJECT, AS ALWAYS; TO THE BOKOR FAMILY FOR WELCOMING US INTO THEIR BEAUTIFUL HOME AND DAILY LIVES; LIZ AND RUSTON FOR EXCELLENT ASSISTANCE AND PERSEVERANCE. THANKS TO ALETA AND RICHARD FOR KEEPING THE PROJECT MOVING. —SUSIE CUSHNER

TABLE OF CONTENTS

INTRODUCTION Everyone always asks how I got started making quilts. My mother was an expert craftsperson and taught me to sew when I was a young girl. I grew up in an area of old New England mill towns and loved to go fabric shopping with her. These early experiences formed the foundation of my interest in textiles and sewing. Before establishing my business, Denyse Schmidt Quilts, I studied graphic design, held many different jobs, and pursued a variety of "careers." At some point (somewhere between sewing bishops' mitres and designing children's books), I developed a passionate appreciation of quilts—especially ones that were a little odd.

The story of quilt making has always been as fascinating to me as the quilts themselves. Some folks may think of quilting as old-fashioned, a hobby your grandmother or great-grandmother enjoyed. But if you look at quilting in a contemporary light, an exciting transformation occurs. For me, that means combining my modern color and design sensibilities with the time-honored traditions of the craft, making something unexpected by juxtaposing new and old.

I essentially taught myself to quilt by reading books and by making more than a few mistakes. I suppose that's where I learned that there is beauty in imperfection. I hope you'll keep that in mind as you create your own quilting projects. Don't stress out about making mistakes. Rather, take advantage of those happy little accidents, and enjoy the process.

It's also helpful to be aware that there are many approaches and techniques used in quilt making. *Denyse Schmidt Quilts* isn't intended to be a comprehensive guide to quilting, and I certainly wouldn't say that my way is the only, or the "correct," way to do things. Once you've developed a healthy obsession with quilting, you'll want to explore many other approaches. The local library, quilt guilds and stores, bookstores, and the Internet are all great places to look for information and inspiration.

The important thing is to *begin.*

No quilting experience is necessary to create the projects in this book. All you'll need are some basic sewing skills. Some of you will prefer following the instructions to the letter, which is fine, and some of you may use this book as a springboard to your own ideas. Either way, it's very important to read through all of the techniques before you begin. You will refer back to them as you make the projects and quilts, but it's a good idea to be familiar with them before you get started. First review the "Tools" and "Fabric and Design" sections (see pages 11 and 12) to discover what materials you'll need. Then, browse through "Project Techniques"

(see page 12) for an overview of the methods you'll be using.

In "Twenty Projects," which begins on page 31, you'll find a range of smaller projects that will introduce you to the concepts of piecing and quilting. If you've never quilted before, this is a good place to start. In "Ten Quilts," which begins on page 107, you'll find some quilt projects that are fast and super simple and others that are more challenging.

One of the great quilt-making traditions is the sharing of designs and ideas. Creating this book is my way of participating in that tradition. If you're new to quilting and patch-work, I hope that this book will help spark a long-term interest. If you're an experienced crafter, I hope that you'll feel inspired by the projects and discover new ways of doing things in the process.

Have fun.

DENYSE SCHMIDT QUILTS

AND YOU CAN TOO!

In this section, you'll find an overview of the tools necessary to complete the projects in this book, as well as some that are optional but helpful. You'll also find information about fabric and quilt design, in addition to basic sewing, quilting, and finishing techniques. If you're an experienced quilter, this section calls out the differences from traditional quilting. If you're just starting out, it's probably a good idea to read through this section to become familiar with the practicalities.

TOOLS

Before you begin a project, review the list of tools below and the "What You Need" sections for the projects you select. If you know how to sew or quilt, you'll probably have many of these items already. Visit sewing, quilting, or craft supply stores for things you are missing. Whenever possible, purchase the best tools you can afford, as all are not created equal. Better tools yield superior results and make the process both easier and more enjoyable. Refer to "Design Aids" on page 12 and "Resources" on page 171 for additional information.

MEASURING, MARKING, AND CUTTING TOOLS

- Acrylic ruler (6 inches by 24 inches; a 4-inch-by-14-inch ruler is also handy, but not essential)
- Tape measure (60 inches or longer for quilts)
- Mechanical pencil with soft leads
- Fabric-marking pencils in white or silver
- Dressmakers' chalk
  Note: Always review the manufacturer's instructions before using a fabric-marking pencil or chalk.
- Powdered chalk and pouncer
- Craft scissors (to cut paper or template materials)
- Embroidery scissors or snips (convenient for cutting threads or small detail work)
- Pinking shears
- Fabric shears
- Utility knife
- Rotary cutter (45mm) and extra blades
- Rotary cutter (28mm) for cutting curves and extra blades
- Rotary cutting mat (at least 18 inches by 24 inches)

TEMPLATE MAKING TOOLS

- Lightweight cardboard (such as file folders) or template plastic
- Rubber cement or glue stick

SEWING AND PRESSING TOOLS

- Glass-head quilting pins (irons can melt plastic heads)
- Needles for general sewing and quilting
- Sewing machine
- Yarn or tapestry needle (for making tied quilts)
- Embroidery needle
- Dual-purpose sewing thread
- Cotton-wrapped polyester quilting thread
- Crochet thread, yarn, and embroidery floss as needed for projects

MISCELLANEOUS SEWING AND FINISHING TOOLS

- Plastic, leather, or metal thimble
- Seam ripper
- Point turner
- Steam iron
- Ironing board
- Large pressing board (see page 18)
- Quilting hoop or frame (not to be confused with an embroidery hoop)
- Teflon foot (for stitching vinyl on your sewing machine)
- Walking foot (for machine-quilting)

HELPFUL DESIGN AIDS

(see page 12 for descriptions)
- Ruby glass
- Window template
- Flannel design wall
- Reducing glass

FABRIC AND DESIGN

FABRIC BASICS

One hundred percent cotton fabric is the best overall choice for patchwork quilts and most of the projects in this book. Washing and normal wear increase its beauty, and over time, the fabric grows softer. You can use light- or medium-weight wools, silks, or blends (in fact, some projects call for these), but for the most part, cotton ensures the best results. All yardages in this book are based on standard 45-inch-wide commercially available quilting cottons, but if you fall in love with a fabric that is wider or narrower, don't let that stop you. Simply alter the yardage to accommodate for the difference.

Pre-washing your cotton fabric can seem like a drag, especially when you're excited about getting started. But don't skip this step. Trim the cut edges of the fabric with pinking shears before washing to prevent the tangled-thread nightmare that can occur in the dryer. Wash the fabric in warm water, then dry it. Remove it before it's completely dry, then press. (Eliminating wrinkles is easier if you work with the fabric while it's still damp.) Press with a steam iron set to "Cotton." Because of shrinkage, your 45-inch-wide cotton may now be up to 3 inches narrower, but the instructions have been written with this in mind.

Most fabrics available today are colorfast, but vintage fabrics may have dyes that run. To dye-test your vintage fabrics before you use them, dip a swatch in a bowl of warm water. If the color bleeds, wash and dry the fabric separately. Then do another swatch test. If the color still bleeds, consider replacing it with an alternative fabric. After you've washed, dried, pressed, and dye-tested the fabric, you may be ready for a nap (or a new hobby). Store the fabric in a closet, covered box, or paper bag until you're ready to use it, as bright light can eventually result in fading.

DESIGN BASICS

Without realizing it, you probably already know a lot about designing with fabric. Every time you select a print top to wear with a pair of pants, for instance, you're combining fabrics with an eye to texture and color. As you create the projects in this book, you'll learn even more. Each quilt or project will inspire you to experiment with combinations of fabrics—light with dark, prints with solids, and so on. As you do so, especially if you replicate the color choices shown in the photographs, you'll find yourself internalizing many of the principles that distinguish these designs. In the end, the best approach is to enjoy the process and not overthink. Here are some basic guidelines to get you started.

Fabrics in solid colors predominate most Denyse Schmidt Quilts (DSQ). Prints or stripes are used for accents, which add depth and personality. Small-scale prints, such as calicos or tiny checks, "read" as a solid from a distance, but viewed up close, add textural interest as well. Medium-scale prints such as floral or geometric designs are more visually active, but keep in mind that using too many together can exhaust the eye. Surround these prints with solid fabrics so their individuality can be appreciated. Reproduction prints, many of which are copies of nineteenth-century designs, are DSQ favorites, and yarn-dyed stripes or paisleys are other fun options. Try to maintain a ratio of about 70 percent solids to 30 percent prints. Though certainly not written in stone, this approach tends to yield balanced designs that are both pleasing and surprising.

Choose color combinations that give you a thrill, a jolt, or even a feeling of serenity. Don't worry too much about "the rules." Instead, experiment by holding one color up to another—no matter what it is. Even if you've been taught, for instance, that red doesn't go with pink or vibrant colors don't look right with muddy ones, give it a try. Your emotional responses will tell you a lot more than your brain will. Some of the most exciting quilts in the DSQ collection comprise unexpected combinations of color.

If you find yourself experiencing too-many-fabrics-to-decide paralysis, try this technique: Cut a swatch from each of the fabrics you're considering for a project or particular pattern piece and place them in a paper bag. Give the bag a shake, and without peeking, pick a swatch, then use it. It's surprising how freeing this technique can be, and you may end up with fabric combinations you love but would never have tried. In addition to shaking up your ideas about color, this exercise can make you feel connected (however obliquely) to quiltmakers from bygone days, when too much choice wasn't an issue.

If, after attempting one or two of the projects, you find yourself eager to experiment further with color, consider buying a color wheel and a book about basic color theory. For more information, see "Resources" on page 171.

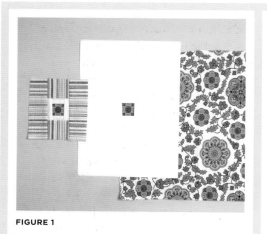

FIGURE 1

DESIGN AIDS

RUBY GLASS

This tool, generally made of red acrylic, helps you identify a fabric's color value (the relative lightness or darkness of a color) by canceling out hues. A hue refers to the quality that gives a color its name. Blue-green is a hue that is somewhere between blue and green on a color continuum. Use the ruby glass if you want to match the values of a print with that of a solid fabric, or if you want to make sure there is enough value contrast or similarity in your selection of fabrics.

WINDOW TEMPLATE

It is easy to make a window template, which is very useful when you are working with large-scale prints. It allows you to locate the perfect texture and/or colors to get the design effect for each pattern piece. Begin by making a copy of the pattern piece and trim off the ¼-inch-wide seam allowance on each side. Center the piece on a sheet of paper and trace around it, then cut out the shape. Move the pattern piece's window over your fabric until you like what you see (Figure 1).

FLANNEL DESIGN WALL

Before stitching your blocks together, you may want to try different arrangements. Hanging up the blocks on a vertical surface lets you stand back and see what your design will look like from a distance. To make this easier, tack a large piece of white flannel to a wall (or, to protect your wall surface, tack it to a foam-core board instead). Cotton quilt blocks will adhere to flannel, so there's no need for pins.

REDUCING GLASS

Getting a sense of the overall design of the quilt can be difficult, because to really see it, you need to be standing a considerable distance away. A reducing glass is the reverse of a magnifying glass and allows you to easily view the design as a whole. In a reduced format, you may spot a design problem, or things that don't seem quite right, that you wouldn't notice when you view a quilt up close. Looking through the wrong end of binoculars or a camera's viewfinder accomplishes the same thing. Try this when you've arranged your quilt blocks on the design wall, before stitching them together, for a different perspective.

FABRIC SHOPPING BASICS

Quilting, craft, and sewing stores are obvious places to find fabric, but don't overlook sources for fun, one-of-a-kind vintage fabrics. A Sunday morning at a flea market can mean the discovery of a tattered box filled with random sewing supplies—including remnants of fabric you'd never find at a retail store. Thrift shops are excellent sources, as well. There you will find racks of inexpensive shirts, dresses, and skirts that can be cut and used for your projects. And, of course, there are always online auctions, where even a low bid might yield a big stash of cotton prints. Make it a habit to consider almost any place as a source for fabric. The same is true for buttons, trim, and notions. While shops that sell new items offer a wide array of choices, more unique things can often be found at tag sales or church bazaars.

For the quilts and some of the other projects in this book, you'll need to buy batting as well. Batting is available at quilting and fabric stores in both cotton and polyester fibers; there is also a range of batting weights from which to choose. You'll learn more about choosing batting on page 20.

PROJECT TECHNIQUES

This section of the book is designed as a resource. Think of it as your tutor. If you have a question while working on a project or quilt, the answer is probably here. If you're new to sewing or patchwork quilting and need to learn some of the basic techniques, you'll find them outlined in the sections that follow. Even if you're an experienced quiltmaker, it's important to read through this section before you begin; after all, the DSQ approach is not always the conventional approach!

Until you are familiar with the techniques, you may often find yourself flipping back to this section of the book. Here's a tip: Photocopy the sections most relevant to your project, and pin them up where you can easily refer to them.

PREPARING THE PATTERN PIECES
FOR THE PATCHWORK PROJECTS

Identify the pattern you will need for your project. The name of the project is printed on each pattern. Enlarge the pattern to the size indicated, and then cut out the enlarged pattern pieces. Each pattern includes ¼-inch-wide seam allowances.

Templates are usually used for making quilts because they withstand the wear and tear of repeated use that comes with making multiple pieces of the same shape. A template's heavy construction also allows you to trace its shape accurately onto fabric. Then you use a rotary cutter and acrylic ruler to cut the shape out of several layers of fabric at one time.

To create templates, enlarge the pattern for your project to the size indicated. Cut the enlarged pattern pieces from the paper, then use rubber cement or a glue stick to glue them to pieces of lightweight cardboard (a file folder works well) or template plastic. Cut out around each pattern piece with a utility knife and a straight-edge or with craft scissors. For a couple of projects, such as "Snake Charmer" (see page 135), you'll need to make mirror-image templates, which is essentially the reverse side of the template. Make an extra copy of the pattern piece, and after cutting it out, glue the *printed* side to the cardboard or template plastic.

Some quilt designs have more than one block pattern, each with several pieces. For at-a-glance identification, color-code the pieces for each block with a marker or sticky dot (for instance, mark all Block 1 pattern pieces with a red dot).

LAYING OUT AND CUTTING

For most of the projects in this book, pattern pieces don't need to be laid out precisely with the grain of the fabric, as they would be when you make clothing. Simply position each piece with the lengthwise or crosswise grain, more or less, and you'll get good results. Slight variations in grain direction will add interest to your quilt or project, which is especially true when you work with stripes or plaids.

That said, be as accurate as you can when cutting out your pieces (both paper and fabric). Tiny fractions of difference can affect the overall finished dimensions of the project. Also, when you're laying out the pieces, don't let them overlap with the selvage edge, as those areas are not usable.

FOR THE PATCHWORK PROJECTS

Arrange the paper pattern pieces right side up on the right side of the fabric. Pin in place. Use fabric shears to cut out each piece. Cut one piece per pattern piece unless otherwise indicated.

FOR THE QUILT PROJECTS

Most quilts are constructed from multiples of each pattern piece. To save time, before laying out your templates, layer the fabric (right side up) to create up to six layers (four layers or fewer if you are new to rotary-cutting). Next, you'll trace the template shapes onto the fabric, then use a rotary cutter and acrylic ruler to cut along the trace lines. To do so, arrange the plastic or cardboard templates right side up on the fabric in groups of roughly the same length, with the long sides meeting and the narrow ends slightly staggered (one up, the next down, and so on) (Figure 2A). Lightly trace around each template with a mechanical pencil; the long side of one template can be shared with the long side of the other to save space. You can shift the neighboring templates slightly as you trace each one (Figure 2B). Tracing the templates onto the fabric in this manner allows you to rotary-cut the long side of one rectangle, for example, while simultaneously cutting the side of a piece next to it. This means you'll make fewer cuts, which saves time, and you'll use a little less fabric. After you've traced the templates for each group, slide the templates off the fabric, keeping them in the same configuration for reference (Figure 2C). Cut apart each group to make it easier to rotary-cut the pieces (Figure 2D). In each group, make the long cuts first (Figure 2E), and then cut the short ends (Figure 2F). As you cut, move each stack of cut pieces to one side and clip the corresponding template to the top of the stack (Figure 2G). If you need to use the template to trace and cut more pieces, pin a piece of paper to the stack indicating the pattern piece and its "right reading" direction (see "Keeping Track of the Fabric Pieces" on page 14).

CUTTING SELVAGE TO SELVAGE

In general, the most efficient way to create borders, bindings, or the layers of rectangles onto which you'll trace your template pieces is to cut several strips, or widths, of a fabric. Fold the fabric so the selvage edges meet ("selvage to selvage") (Figure 3A).

Position the fabric on your cutting mat with the folded edge facing you and aligned with the mat's grid. The selvage edges should also align with the mat's grid, parallel to the folded edge. When cutting strips or widths from folded fabric, it's important that your cuts be perpendicular to the fold line, so that when you unfold the strip, the sides will be straight. A cut that is not perpendicular to the fold line will result in a strip that is bent at its fold line. Using the measurement lines on your ruler and mat as a guide, cut the strips to the measurement required, rolling the cutter away from you, beginning at the fold and ending at the selvage edges (Figure 3B). When you open up the strips, each end will be a selvage edge. If you're using the complete strip (as a border or stripe), trim off the selvage edges using the grids on the

FIGURE 2A

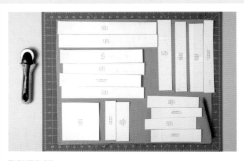

FIGURE 2B

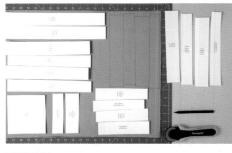

FIGURE 2C

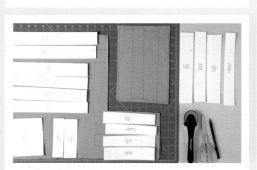

FIGURE 2D

FIGURE 2E

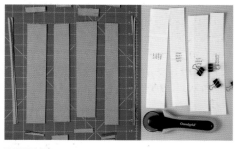

FIGURE 2F

FIGURE 2G

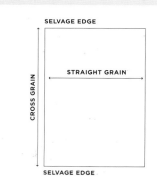

SELVAGE EDGE

STRAIGHT GRAIN

CROSS GRAIN

SELVAGE EDGE

FIGURE 3A

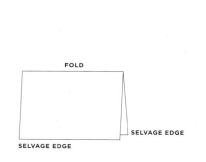

FOLD

SELVAGE EDGE

SELVAGE EDGE

ruler and cutting mat as a guide. Note that the selvage area of the fabric should not be used in a project. Its weave and texture are not the same as the rest of the fabric. In all cases you will either not use the selvage edges or you will trim them off.

KEEPING TRACK OF THE FABRIC PIECES
READY-SET-SEW

When it comes to a Denyse Schmidt patchwork block, a square is not always an exact square. Several irregular shapes with not-quite-straight lines are designed to fit together (think of a jigsaw puzzle) to create a somewhat less-than-perfect square. For this reason, you must arrange your pieces, after they have been cut, in precisely the same arrangement as they will be stitched. To make this easier, the text and numerals on the patterns have been designed to be "right reading" in the Ready-Set-Sew position (Figure 4A). In other words, the text will always be oriented so that you can read it left to right when the pattern pieces are positioned correctly (Figure 4B). Always use the pattern text as a guide to position the pieces.

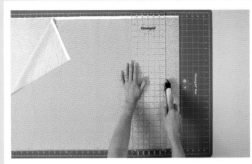

FIGURE 3B

USING A ROTARY CUTTER

Rotary-cutting is speedy and results in clean, precise lines. But if you are new to this method of cutting, it's important to practice first and keep the following tips in mind:

- *Be sure your rotary blade is new or sharp so it will easily make a clean cut. Keep extra blades on hand.*

- *Be sure the edges of your acrylic ruler do not have any nicks, as this will cause your cut lines to be uneven and prevent the rotary-cutting blade from rolling smoothly along the edge.*

- *Transparent dots or sheets with adhesive backing secured to the bottom of your ruler can help prevent it from shifting. Otherwise, use a ruler with a non-slip surface.*

- *Before you begin, unlock the rotary cutter's safety mechanism. Between cuts, secure the lock. An exposed blade on a table heaped with fabric can lead to accidents.*

- *Always roll the cutter away from your body in a single continuous motion. To change the direction of the cut line, rotate your cutting mat rather than cutting side to side or toward your body.*

- *When cutting straight lines, use your acrylic ruler as a guide. Keep the blade perpendicular to and snug against the edge of the ruler. Use your pinky and ring fingers to help brace the ruler by extending them onto the fabric opposite the side you are cutting.*

- *Rotary blades are very sharp and can easily cut through several layers of fabric without excessive force! Use gentle pressure on the cutter, and maintain a firm, consistent hold on the ruler.*

FIGURE 4A

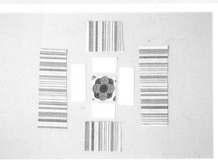

FIGURE 4B

THE COMPASS PIN

As you stitch together your fabric pieces, you'll naturally turn around what you are sewing to attach each new piece. It's easy to forget which side is which when you return your block or strip to the Ready-Set-Sew position. To avoid getting "lost," place a pin in the Center Square (see "Modified–Log Cabin Method" on this page) or in the left-hand strip (see "String-Piecing Method" on page 16) with the point of the pin away from you, or pointing "north." Think of the pin as a compass needle: When you lose track of the sides, turn your work until the pin faces "north" again.

ASSEMBLING THE PATCHWORK PIECES

There are two basic piecing methods for nearly all the patchwork projects and quilts in this book. Modified–Log Cabin takes its

inspiration from its traditional namesake, the Log Cabin. Its blocks is composed of fabric strips (the cabin's logs) that are stitched around a fabric center (the cabin's fireplace or hearth). The "String-Piecing Method" described on page 16 is also based on a traditional construction method, where strips of fabric are sewn together to create quilt blocks or long rows. "Foundation-Piecing" is another construction method, though the basic piecing order follows either the String-Piecing Method or the Modified–Log Cabin Method. In the Foundation-Piecing Method, the pieces get stitched to a foundation, rather than to each other.

MODIFIED–LOG CABIN METHOD

Creating these quilt blocks is like building a square from the inside out. Envision a four-sided frame constructed around a center square. Next, visualize an additional frame, this one wrapping around the first. The more frames you add, the greater the size of your quilt block. But whether you add one frame or several, the basic rules for construction remain the same: Stitch the short sides of a frame first and the long sides next, unless the instructions indicate otherwise.

1 - Arrange the pieces in the "Ready-Set-Sew" position (see page 14). Place a pin in the Center Square, with the point facing "north." This is your Compass Pin (Figure 5A).

2 - With right sides together, sew the first frame: Stitch A-Top to the upper edge of the Center Square, then A-Bottom to the lower edge of the Center Square. Press the seams outward from the Center Square, toward the A pieces (Figure 5B).

3 - With right sides together, continue by stitching A-Left to the left side of the Center Square and A-Right to the right side of the Center Square. Press the seams outward, toward the A pieces (Figure 5C).

4 - Sew the second frame: Repeat Step 2, but this time stitch the B-Top and B-Bottom pieces to the A-Top and A-Bottom pieces. Press the seams outward toward the B pieces. Then stitch B-Left and B-Right to A-Left and A-Right pieces, pressing seams outward (Figure 5D).

5 - If your block requires more frames, continue in the same manner, following the Ready-Set-Sew stitching order.

STRING-PIECING METHOD

Imagine a rectangular piece or strip, and then imagine a row of them, stitched together to create a wider piece of fabric. To avoid confusing the pieces, which can look alike, always stitch your pieces together from left to right. Rather than press each seam as you stitch, sew all the pieces together first, then press all the seams at the same time.

1 - Arrange the pieces in the "Ready-Set-Sew" position (see page 14). Place a pin in the left-hand piece, with the point facing "north." This is your Compass Pin (Figure 6A).

2 - With right sides together, stitch A to B (Figure 6B), then stitch B to C (Figure 6C), then C to D, and so on, until you've stitched together all the panels or strips. Press all the seams to one side or as indicated in the project instructions (Figure 6D).

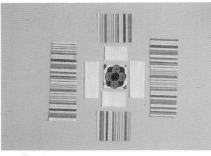

FIGURE 5A

FIGURE 6A

FIGURE 5B

FIGURE 6B

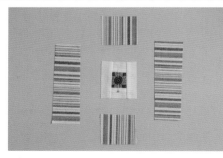

FIGURE 5C

FIGURE 6C

FIGURE 5D

FIGURE 6D

FIGURE 7A   FIGURE 7B   FIGURE 7C   FIGURE 7D   FIGURE 7E

FOUNDATION-PIECING METHOD

Foundation-Piecing, just as its name suggests, is traditionally worked on a piece of paper or fabric, which becomes the foundation. Scraps or strips of fabric are stitched directly to this foundation piece, rather than to each other (such as in the Modified–Log Cabin Method or String-Piecing Method). Foundation-Piecing has the advantage of added stability when working with very lightweight or delicate fabrics such as silk or when mixing lightweight fabrics with heavier-weight fabrics such as wool. In addition, Foundation-Piecing facilitates designs that are more improvisational (creating a design without patterns) or that require a high degree of precision.

1 - With the foundation fabric (muslin or lightweight cotton) flat on your working surface, arrange your cut strips in a row as follows: Lay the first strip, right side up, flush with the outer left-hand edge of the foundation piece. Depending on the size of your work, you may wish to pin it in place. Stitch the strip to the foundation along the outer edge, backstitching at both ends to secure the stitches (Figure 7A).

2 - Working left to right, position a new strip, with right sides together and the right edges aligned, on top of the first (Figure 7B). Stitch through all the layers along the right-hand edge with a ¼-inch-wide seam allowance. Press flat, then press the second strip to the right (Figure 7C).

3 - Repeat Step 2 with a new strip, and continue in this fashion until you have covered the foundation fabric. Press.

4 - Turn the project over (strip side down) and square up your block (see "Squaring Up" on page 29) to the size indicated in the project instructions (Figure 7D).

5 - Machine-baste around the perimeter of the project, ⅛ inch from the edges (Figure 7E).

Create a large work surface that doubles as a pressing board. A board like this is portable, so when you're not using it, you can slip it into a closet or under a bed. To make the pressing board, have a home improvement or hardware store cut a piece of plywood to about 4 feet by 4 feet (plus or minus, depending on your needs and available space). Place three 4 1/2-foot-by-4 1/2-foot layers of batting on top of the plywood. Then place a piece of muslin (slightly larger than 4 1/2 feet by 4 1/2 feet) on top of the batting. Pull the edges to the back of the board, and staple-gun in place. Before placing the board on your dining table or desk, protect the surface with a pad or some extra layers of batting.

PRESSING

Set your iron to "Cotton" with the steam feature on. Press down on the fabric, lifting the iron to move to the next area before pressing down again. Do not move the iron back and forth across the fabric because this may stretch or distort your blocks. Seams should be pressed "flat" first (Figure 8A), then pressed again to one side (Figure 8B).

In general, seams should be pressed outward from the center or toward the darker fabric. The project instructions will usually tell you what direction to press your seams, but you can also let the seam allowance be your guide. The seam will tend to lean one way or the other, especially if one of the sides has intersecting seams in it or if one fabric is heavier than another (Figure 8C). Press it in the direction that it's leaning naturally. You may find with some quilts that pressing the row seams as prescribed isn't always possible—for instance, when a block edge has a few or more seams perpendicular to that edge. If you have a seam allowance that won't easily press in the direction you want it to go, don't fight it. A couple of bulky corners won't ruin your project. Just avoid marking any hand-quilting lines through that corner.

FIGURE 8A

FIGURE 8B

FIGURE 8C

CONSTRUCTING A QUILT

In this section you'll find everything you need to know to complete the projects in "Ten Quilts," which begins on page 107. Creating a quilt requires time, but it is not difficult. In fact, the process is relatively simple. A quilt typically consists of three layers: the Quilt Top, the batting in the middle, and the Quilt Back. The project instructions show you how to make the elements for each Quilt Top, and this section tells you how to put it all together. Begin by reading through the instructions for each quilt project and the techniques in this section, and refer back as you need to. And remember, the years of use and enjoyment you will get from your quilt will more than repay your investment of time and effort.

CHOOSING A QUILT SIZE

The quilts in this book are sized with about a 13-inch-long drop on the sides and foot, which works well for a platform bed or with a bed skirt. You may wish to modify the size of a quilt to fit your own bed. Below is a chart showing standard mattress sizes and the approximate dimensions of each size quilt. To size the quilt for your own bed, you'll need to determine what size your quilt should be to get the look you want. Do you want it to hang to the floor? If so, how high is the top of the mattress? Do you want it to go over the pillows with a tuck? You'll need to add to the length. The best way to figure this out is to use a tape measure. Once you've determined the size you want your quilt to be, note the dimensions listed in the instructions for the quilt you are making. To make a quilt larger, you can add rows of blocks, or eliminate them to make it smaller. You can also gain inches by adding strips of fabric between blocks (called lattice strips or sashing) or by adding a border. Remember to include seam allowances in your calculations.

	STANDARD MATTRESS SIZE	DSQ STANDARD QUILT SIZE
CRIB	27 inches by 52 inches	40 inches by 50 inches
TWIN	38 inches by 74 inches	64 inches by 87 inches
FULL	54 inches by 74 inches	80 inches by 87 inches
QUEEN	60 inches by 80 inches	86 inches by 93 inches
KING	76 inches by 80 inches	102 inches by 93 inches

Figures

BLOCK 1A	BLOCK 1B	BLOCK 1C	BLOCK 1D
BLOCK 2A	BLOCK 2B	BLOCK 2C	BLOCK 2D
BLOCK 3A	BLOCK 3B	BLOCK 3C	BLOCK 3D
BLOCK 4A	BLOCK 4B	BLOCK 4C	BLOCK 4D
BLOCK 5A	BLOCK 5B	BLOCK 5C	BLOCK 5D

FIGURE 9A

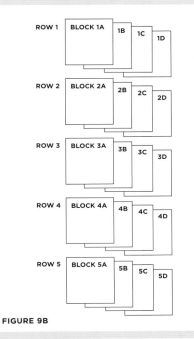

ROW 1 — BLOCK 1A, 1B, 1C, 1D
ROW 2 — BLOCK 2A, 2B, 2C, 2D
ROW 3 — BLOCK 3A, 3B, 3C, 3D
ROW 4 — BLOCK 4A, 4B, 4C, 4D
ROW 5 — BLOCK 5A, 5B, 5C, 5D

FIGURE 9B

BLOCK 1A	BLOCK 1B	BLOCK 1C	BLOCK 1D
BLOCK 2A	BLOCK 2B	BLOCK 2C	BLOCK 2D
BLOCK 3A	BLOCK 3B	BLOCK 3C	BLOCK 3D
BLOCK 4A	BLOCK 4B	BLOCK 4C	BLOCK 4D
BLOCK 5A	BLOCK 5B	BLOCK 5C	BLOCK 5D

FIGURE 9C

ASSEMBLING THE QUILT TOP

After you've stitched the pattern pieces together to make all the blocks for your quilt project, you'll arrange the blocks to create the overall quilt design. Then you'll be ready to move to the sewing machine to stitch all the blocks together—a rewarding experience!

ARRANGE THE QUILT BLOCKS

To arrange the quilt blocks before stitching them together, lay them out on the floor or use a flannel design wall (see page 12). Refer to the photograph and instructions for the quilt you are making, or arrange the blocks to make your own unique design. If you'd like to experiment with block placement, now is the time to do so.

MOVE 'EM TO THE MACHINE

Once you've arranged the blocks, you're ready to stitch them together. This isn't difficult, but it's helpful to have a system for removing the blocks from the wall or floor and moving them to the sewing machine. You don't want to undo all your design efforts by stitching the blocks together incorrectly. It's frustrating to have to rip out and re-stitch seams, especially when you're so close to finishing your Quilt Top! Here's how we do it at DSQ: From scrap paper, make a label for each quilt block. Label the blocks as shown in the diagram, with rows from top to bottom numbered 1, 2, 3, and so on, and rows left to right labeled A, B, C, and so on (Figure 9A). For example, the top left corner block is Block 1A, the one to the right of it Block 1B, etc. Write all the labels you'll need, and pin each to its corresponding block at the top center of the block. Then, remove the blocks from the wall or floor one row at a time, working left to right. To remove Row 1, stack Block 1A on top of Block 1B, Block 1B on top of Block 1C, and so on until you've stacked all the Row 1 blocks (Figure 9B). Set the Row 1 stack aside, then remove and stack all the other rows in the same manner. When you're done, you can re-use the labels for your next quilt project. Now you are ready to stitch!

BLOCKS INTO ROWS

With right sides together, stitch the rows together as follows: Sew the right edge of the A Block to the left edge of the B Block, then the right edge of the B Block to the left edge of C Block. Continue in this manner, and stitch all the blocks in each row together. Press the seams in odd rows to the left and the seams in the even rows to the right. This will reduce seam allowance bulk at the point where four blocks meet.

STITCH THE ROWS TOGETHER

Now you're ready to sew the rows together. With right sides together and block seams aligned, stitch the bottom of Row 1 to the top of Row 2, the bottom of Row 2 to the top of Row 3, and so on until you've sewn all the rows together (Figure 9C). Press the seams to one side. Congratulations! You've completed your Quilt Top.

PLANNING YOUR QUILTING

The next step in making your quilt is to mark the Quilt Top for hand- or machine-quilting or for tying. The quilting or tying is what holds the three layers of your quilt together. Tied quilts are usually marked out in an all-over grid pattern, sometimes using the block seam lines as a guide (see "Any Way You Slice It" on page 125). Hand- or machine-quilting can be done in either an all-over pattern, meaning the design of the quilting is independent of the piecing (see "Ice Pops" on page 121), or by outlining the shapes made by the piecing or design of the Quilt Top (see "Drunk Love 2-Tone" on page 151 and the next section on Outline Quilting). You can even use a combination of both styles of quilting (see "Pie in the Sky" on page 145). All the quilt projects in this book include a suggested method and design for this in the instructions. You can quilt or tie your project as suggested, or you can substitute any of the other methods, described in "Joining the Layers" (this page), to finish your project.

OUTLINE QUILTING

There are two common forms of outline quilting: stitch-in-the-ditch and echo quilt-ing. Both are used to accentuate the shape of a quilt block design or appliqué motif. In both cases, the quilting stitches are worked around the perimeter of each shape you want to highlight. In this book, echo quilt-ing is assumed when references to quilting around shapes is made. Specific recom-mendations for stitching-in-the-ditch are mentioned in the project text.

ECHO QUILTING

Traditionally, echo quilting is worked about ¼ inch from the seam line of each shape that requires outlining. The adaptation in this book is worked about 1¼ inches from the seam line or stitch line.

STITCH-IN-THE-DITCH QUILTING

The word "ditch," in this case, refers to the indentation created by the seams that join quilt blocks or borders. To quilt, stitch very close to the seam line, on the side that does not have the seam allowance directly underneath.

MARKING THE QUILTING LINES

Mark the Quilt Top *before* you make the quilt sandwich. To begin marking the quilt-ing lines, refer to the quilt-marking step in the quilt project instructions and use a fab-ric-marking pencil or chalk to mark the de-sign on the Quilt Top. Stitch-in-the-ditch quilting lines do not need to be marked.

Always remember to test pencils and chalks on a fabric swatch according to the manufacturer's instructions. You don't want your marked quilt lines to be permanent.

THE QUILT BACK

If you are making a bed-size quilt, you can back it with a single piece of extra-wide fabric made specifically for Quilt Backs or piece together lengths of narrower fabric. You can also piece together leftover fabric from the Quilt Top. A quick way to create a Quilt Back is to use a pre-washed, 100 percent cotton bedsheet. Choose fabrics in coordinating or complementary colors. To determine the dimensions of the Quilt Back, measure your Quilt Top, then add 5 inches each to the length and width.

SELECTING THE BATTING

Batting comes in a variety of different weights and types, and is sold both as yardage on rolls and in pre-cut bed-size pieces (crib, twin, full, etc.). The weight or type you choose depends on the look you prefer and on how you plan to finish the quilt. A thin to medium-weight cotton batting is the preferred choice of DSQ, as it is easy to hand-quilt and results in a flatter, more "old-fashioned" look. If you plan to tie your quilt, use batting with more loft, such as a polyester batting. To determine the dimensions of the batting, measure your Quilt Top, then add 5 inches each to the length and width.

MAKING THE QUILT SANDWICH

With the wrong side up, smooth the Quilt Back on your work surface or floor, and tape it in place, first lengthwise, then widthwise. For best results, keep the back taut, to re-duce the chance of it wrinkling or bunching up while you baste the layers. (If you are working on a rug or carpet, you can pin it directly to the pile.) Center the batting on top of the Quilt Back and smooth it out, working from the center to the outer edges. With the right side up, center the Quilt Top on the batting, and smooth it flat from the center to the outer edges.

JOINING THE LAYERS
HAND-BASTING

After you have assembled the quilt sand-wich, the next step is to baste the layers to-gether to prevent them from shifting during quilting or tying. You can secure the layers with special basting pins (similar to safety pins) or by basting with needle and thread (see "Hand-Basting Stitch" on page 21). When hand-basting the quilt sandwich, use long running stitches (one every few inches). Your stitch lines should be about

- *Make sure your machine is clean, oiled, and in good working order.*

- *Use a new needle for each project—and use the correct size needle for the thread you select.*

- *Use good-quality thread, and if possible, use threads that are specifically made for machine-quilting.*

- *Use a walking foot.*

- *Unless otherwise suggested in the quilt instructions, start in the middle of the quilt and stitch toward the outer edge. Begin by stitching in place to lock the quilting line. Gradually increase the stitch length to about 8 to 10 stitches per inch.*

- *Practice, practice, practice! A good way to warm up for machine-quilting a quilt is to make the "Too Hot to Handle Oven Mitt" on page 73. Or, practice by making a few 15-inch-by-15-inch "quilt sandwiches" with muslin and pieces of batting, and stitch away!*

FIGURE 10

6 to 8 inches apart. For best results, baste the quilt from the center out. First stitch diagonal lines from the center out to the corners, and then stitch vertical and horizontal lines (Figure 10). Eventually, you will remove the basting. But before then, you will need to hand-quilt, hand-tie, or machine-quilt your quilt. Refer to your quilt project instructions to find out which method we used to finish the quilt (or, if you prefer, choose one of the methods below). Remove the basting stitches after you have finished quilting your quilt.

HAND-QUILTING

Hand-quilting is beautiful because it adds gentle texture and dimension to the otherwise flat surface. Keep in mind that hand-quilting isn't difficult, but it does take time. If you like the look, but don't have time, you can have your project quilted for you by a professional. Inquire at your local quilt shop or quilt guild about quiltmakers who offer this service in your area, or see "Resources" on page 171.

HAND-BASTING STITCH

Hand-basted stitches temporarily hold layers of fabric, or fabric and batting, together prior to quilting, tying, or appliqué. This stitch is typically worked in contrasting thread so you can easily see the stitches when it comes time to remove them. Make generous stitches, about ⅜ inch to ¾ inch long, depending on the size of your project. If you run out of thread as you stitch, don't bother to knot a new piece. Simply rethread the needle and continue, leaving a short tail of thread where you left off.

HAND-QUILTING STITCH

If you are familiar with the running stitch (see page 26), you'll find that the quilting stitch is very similar. Denyse Schmidt Quilts are usually worked in off-white thread, no matter what color the Quilt Top is. If you are new to quilting, it's a good idea to use matching thread, so inconsistencies in your stitching "disappear" into the fabric. Use hand-quilting thread, which won't tangle or fray as easily as all-purpose thread. Aim to create a series of evenly spaced stitches of more or less equal length on both the front and the back. With practice, your stitches will become shorter and more consistent, and you will be able to work more quickly, but don't hold yourself to impossible standards. Using a quilting hoop (not to be confused with its lightweight cousin, the embroidery hoop) can make stitching easier, though some quiltmakers prefer to quilt without it. When you use a hoop, don't pull the quilt as tight as a drum. The fabric should be smooth and taut on both the top and bottom, with enough slack so that you are able to manipulate the fabric while quilting.

1 - Thread a quilting needle with a 15-inch length of hand-quilting thread and make a small knot at the end. (Also refer to "Threading Up" on page 20.) Hide the knot by inserting the needle into your Quilt Top about an inch from your starting point, through some of the batting in the layer beneath (not through the Quilt Back), then push the needle back up to the top to the place where you want to start stitching your design (Figure 11A). Gently tug on the thread until the knot pops through the Quilt Top and you feel the knot lodge in the batting. The trick is to make the knot small enough to pass through the Quilt Top, yet large enough so that it will be buried in the batting.

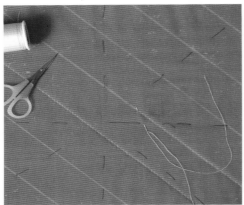

FIGURE 11A

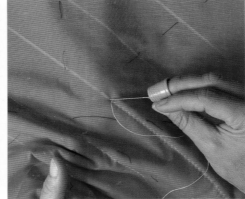

FIGURE 11B

FIGURE 11C

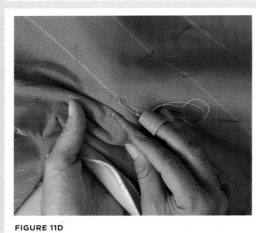

FIGURE 11D

FIGURE 11E

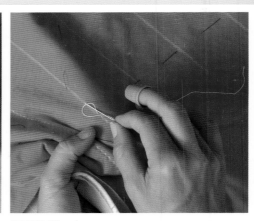

FIGURE 11F

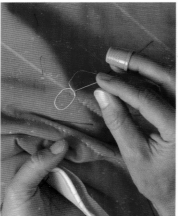

FIGURE 11G

FIGURE 11H

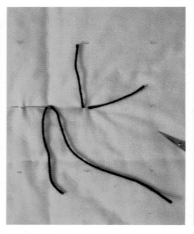

FIGURE 12A

FIGURE 12B

2 - Turn the quilt so that the markings are running at a comfortable angle. Place a thimble on the middle finger of your stitching hand. Holding one hand beneath the work and using the hand with the thimble to stitch, insert the needle down through the Quilt Top just far enough so you feel the point of the needle with one of your fingers underneath (Figure 11B). Catch the fabric of the Quilt Back and pass the needle back up through the Quilt Top, using the finger underneath to push the quilt up slightly at the stitch (Figure 11C). Repeat, and "stack" one or two more stitches on the needle (Figure 11D) before pulling the thread all the way through (Figure 11E). You'll find that the process of stacking stitches onto the needle has a slight rocking motion, which is why this stitch is often called the "rocker stitch." Though it may seem awkward at first, this rocking motion will help you develop a rhythm that results in more even stitches.

3 - Continue, following your markings, until your thread gets short, about 4 or 5 inches in length. Make a loop with the thread, and pass the needle up through the loop (Figure 11F). Hold the point of the needle on the surface of the Quilt Top, about ¼ inch away from where your last stitch ended and inside the loop (Figure 11G). Pull the thread to make the loop smaller, and a knot will form at the point of the needle (Figure 11H). Insert the needle through the Quilt Top as you would for another stitch, but skim through the batting for about 1 inch (without going through to the back) before coming up through the Quilt Top again. Pull on the thread until the knot pops through the Quilt Top. Snip the thread close to the quilt's surface. Thread your needle and start again at Step 1.

MACHINE-QUILTING

Machine-stitching is another way to secure the three layers of a quilt. Some of the quilt projects in this book are machine-quilted, and all of them are done in an all-over figure-eight pattern. The options for stitched designs are the same as those for hand-quilting—outline quilting, echo quilting, stitch-in-the-ditch quilting, or an all-over pattern (see page 20).

If you don't have previous experience and a walking foot for your sewing machine, you might consider alternative methods, such as hand-tying or hand-quilting. To do the figure eight or other patterns with tight curves, you'll need to have experience with free-motion quilting. Or, you can have your project quilted for you by a professional. Inquire at your local quilt shop or quilt guild about quiltmakers who offer this service in your area, or refer to "Resources" on page 171. Finally, if you decide that would like to explore machine-quilting further, refer to "Resources" for book recommendations. (See also page 21 for "Machine-Quilting Tips.")

HAND-TYING

This method, which is easy to do, takes far less time than hand- or machine-quilting. Yarn or crochet thread is knotted at intervals all over the quilt, and these knots hold the three layers of the quilt sandwich together. Use a medium-weight thread or yarn so you can easily stitch through all the layers. Before you begin tying, use your acrylic ruler and fabric-marking pencil or dressmakers' chalk to mark the intervals with small dots.

1 - Thread a needle with an 18-inch length of yarn or crochet thread. *Do not* knot the ends. Insert the needle into the Quilt Top at one of the marks and push the needle through all three layers, leaving a 2-inch-long tail.

2 - Bring the needle back up through the Quilt Top about ¼ inch away from where you entered. Snip the yarn to 2 inches (Figure 12A). Tie the ends together using a square knot (right over left, then left over right). Trim the ends to about ¾ to 1 inch long.

3 - Repeat Steps 1 and 2, making ties at every marked interval.

SPEEDY HAND-TYING

Here is a speedier version of hand-tying: Cut a 24-inch (or longer if you like) piece of yarn, work as in Steps 1 and 2, but don't snip the yarn between stitches. Instead, leave about 4-inch-long loops between stitches (Figure 12B). Continue in this manner until you run out of yarn or floss. Snip all the loops and tie the ends, as in Step 2. Repeat with another length of yarn or crochet thread, until you have made all the ties at each marked interval.

SEAM ALLOWANCE JARGON

If a project calls for a scant seam allowance, make it a tiny bit narrower than the measurement stated. A generous seam allowance is a tiny bit wider than the measurement stated.

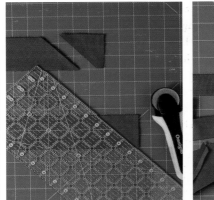

FIGURE 13A

FIGURE 13B

FIGURE 13C

FIGURE 13D

FIGURE 13E

FIGURE 13F

FIGURE 13G

FIGURE 13H

FIGURE 13I

FIGURE 13J

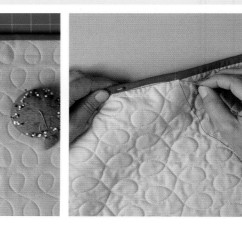

FIGURE 13K

FIGURE 13L

Lay out the binding on the Quilt Top before stitching it in place. Be sure the seams of the binding won't fall at the corners, as this will add bulk to the corners.

BINDING THE QUILT

The binding finishes the raw edges of a quilt. As with most aspects of quilt making, there are many methods used to do this. The quilts in this book are bound using a double-fold, cross-grain technique with "mitered" corners, which results in a $3/8$-inch-wide edging on the front and back and square corners. Most of the sewing is done with a sewing machine, but the final step requires hand-stitching. Before adding the binding, trim the batting and Quilt Back so they are even with the Quilt Top. Then make sure the sides of your quilt are straight and all corners are square (see "Squaring Up" on page 29).

1 - Begin with a little arithmetic. Compute the perimeter measurement of your quilt by adding the width to the length and multiplying it by two. Divide that measurement by the width of your binding fabric. Don't include selvages in your measurement. The number you are left with determines the number of strips of fabric you will need to cut. Add an extra 18 inches to the total, to allow for seaming the strips together, turning corners, and finishing the ends, then round up to the next whole number. (If, for example, you need a little more than five strips, cut six strips.) Each strip should measure $2\frac{1}{2}$ inches wide.

2 - To cut the strips, refer to "Cutting Selvage to Selvage" on page 13.

3 - Stack the folded cut strips (up to four). Using the grid on your cutting mat as a guide, make 45-degree angle cuts at the ends (Figure 13A). With right sides together, stitch the strips end to end to create one long strip. Press seams open.

4 - With *wrong* sides together, fold the seamed strips in half lengthwise and press. Trim the points from the seam allowances (Figure 13B).

5 - Starting in the center of one side, rather than at a corner (and leaving about 8 inches free for joining the ends later), align the raw edge of the folded binding with the raw edge of the Quilt Top. With a scant $3/8$-inch-wide seam allowance, stitch the binding to the quilt, stopping $3/8$ inch short of the first corner. Backstitch. Remove the quilt and binding from under the needle, and snip the threads (Figure 13C).

6 - Fold the loose end of the binding toward the right (Figure 13D). Then, fold the binding back toward the left, with the edge of the fold aligned with the stitched side and the raw edge aligned with the second side of the quilt (Figure 13E). Pin in place.

7 - Starting $3/8$ inch from the edge, backstitch without catching the folds of the binding, and then stitch along the second side with a $3/8$-inch-wide seam allowance (Figure 13F). Repeat for the remaining sides.

8 - When you are about 12 inches from the beginning of the binding, stop stitching. Unfold the ends of the binding, and lay the end you just stitched flat along the edge of the quilt. Lay the beginning end of the binding on top of the other strip. Using chalk, mark where the beginning end intersects the strip beneath it (Figure 13G). Mark the same 45-degree angle on the bottom strip, adding $\frac{1}{2}$ inch beyond the chalk mark for the seam allowance (Figure 13H). Trim the bottom strip along the 45-degree angle (Figure 13I). With right sides together, stitch the ends on the diagonal and press the seam open (Figure 13J). Refold, trim the points, and finish stitching the binding to the quilt.

9 - Fold the binding over the raw edge toward the Quilt Back with a $3/8$-inch width of binding showing on both the front and back. Pin (Figure 13K). Blindstitch the binding in place, just covering the seam line (Figure 13L).

BASIC SEWING SKILLS: A REFERENCE

Here's a quick reference to use if you come across an unfamiliar stitch type in the project or quilt instructions.

MACHINE-SEWING

SEAM ALLOWANCES

Unless otherwise indicated, use ¼-inch-wide seam allowances. Try to keep your seam allowance consistent. A fraction of an inch, multiplied across many pieces, can add up. Your shapes could end up larger, smaller, or more angled than you want them to be.

One way to ensure a straight seam allowance is to attach a patchwork presser foot (sometimes called a ¼-inch foot), which is designed for just this purpose, to your sewing machine. If you don't have a patchwork foot, do this to create a seam guide: Measure ¼ inch to the right of your needle, then mark the distance with a piece of masking tape secured to your sewing machine plate.

BACKSTITCH

Make it a rule to backstitch at the beginning and end of each seam. A few stitches in reverse can make a difference between a project that holds together beautifully and one that eventually comes apart.

REMOVING STITCHES

If you are unsatisfied with one of your seams, use a seam ripper to remove the stitches, and then start again. Be sure to rip the threads carefully, as you don't want to damage the fabric. Remove the threads after ripping so they don't get caught up in the next seams that you stitch.

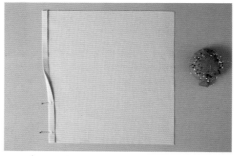

FIGURE 14

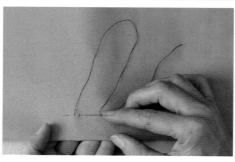

FIGURE 15

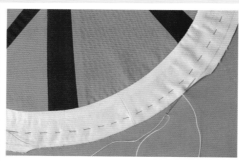

FIGURE 16

FIGURE 17

DOUBLE-TURN HEM

To prevent the raw edges of your fabric from fraying or unraveling—and to finish the edges—turn up ¼ inch (or the amount specified in the project instructions), then turn up a second ¼ inch (Figure 14). Sew a straight stitch through both layers, backstitching at the beginning and end of the seam. Press the finished edges.

EDGESTITCH

The edgestitch is used to keep a seam allowance from rolling, to keep an edge flat, or to strengthen seams. Stitch about ⅛ inch or closer from the finished edge or seam.

TOPSTITCH

The topstitch is used to secure seams, attach pockets, or add a decorative finish. This stitch is worked on the right side, about ¼ inch away from an edge or seam, through all the layers.

STAY STITCH

The stay stitch isn't used to seam two pieces together. Rather, it is used to prevent curves from stretching or shapes from distorting. It is stitched about ⅛ inch from the seam line *inside* the seam allowance.

HAND-SEWING

RUNNING STITCH

The running stitch is the most basic of all the stitches—and it has many uses. With a threaded needle, take several small forward stitches, evenly weaving the needle in and out of the fabric layers. Before pulling the thread through, pick up as many stitches as your needle and fabric will allow. For permanent seams, make stitches about 1/16 inch to ⅛ inch long.

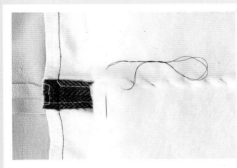

FIGURE 18

BACKSTITCH

The backstitch is used to make strong hand-sewn seams or for decorative stitches. Bring your threaded needle up through the fabric at your starting point. Then insert the point of the needle about $1/8$ inch behind where the thread comes out from the previous stitch, and bring it up again about $1/8$ inch in front of the thread. Pull the thread through to make the stitch. Your next stitch behind the thread will just meet the end of your last stitch (Figure 15). Continue to make even, $1/8$-inch-long stitches behind and in front of the thread from the previous stitch to create an unbroken line of stitching.

BLIND STITCH

The benefit of this hand-stitch is that it is almost invisible. Use it for appliqué or to finish binding quilts. To blindstitch, slide the needle up through the bottom fabric, and pick up a thread or two of the folded edge of the top fabric before taking the next stitch, as shown (Figure 16). Take $1/8$-inch-long stitches for an invisible finish.

SLIP STITCH

This is a concealed stitch that is often used to sew folded edges together to close seam openings or for hems. It can also be used to finish binding quilts. With the fold of the hem toward you, take even, $1/8$-inch-long stitches on the inside of the fold edges, alternating between the two sides (Figure 17).

WHIPSTITCH

The whipstitch consists of slanted stitches that are used to hold two edges together. Hold the needle at right angles to the edge to take the stitches. For stitches that will be visible, make them even and about $1/8$ inch long. For a whipstitch that will be hidden, you can take more generous $1/4$-inch-long stitches (Figure 18).

APPLIQUÉ

Instructions for the needle-turn appliqué method are provided here. The projects that use appliqué in this book have rounded shapes, and needle-turn is a good method to use to produce smooth curves. You'll use your needle to turn under the seam allowance as you stitch and the blind stitch to secure the motif to the background fabric. Choose a thread color that matches the piece you are appliquéing. There are many other methods for appliqué, however—adapt the project instructions to use the method that works best for you. For an appliqué book recommendation, refer to "Resources" on page 171.

1 - With a pencil, lightly mark a line $1/8$ to $3/16$ inch from the edge of the motif on the right side of the fabric. For smaller shapes, use the smaller measurement; for larger shapes, use the larger measurement. You can use your acrylic ruler to make a series of dots along the edge, and then connect the dots to draw the line.

2 - Pin the motif in place on the background fabric. For larger motifs, it's a good idea to hand-baste the motif directly to the background fabric before you appliqué.

3 - Thread your needle with a 15-inch length of quilting thread, and knot the end.

4 - Use your needle to fold under the seam allowance of the appliqué motif at your starting point. Bring your threaded needle up through the background fabric, exactly in line with the folded edge of the appliqué, and catch a couple of threads on the edge of the appliqué fold. Pull the thread through, making sure the stitch holding the appliqué piece is taut (Figure 19A).

5 - Insert the needle into the background fabric next to the stitch in the appliqué fold (Figure 19B). Slide the needle under the background fabric about $1/8$ inch, and come up again exactly in line with the folded edge of the appliqué, catching another couple threads on the edge of the appliqué fold (Figure 19C). As you stitch, use the point of the needle to turn under the edge along the pencil line.

6 - Continue stitching and work your way around the appliqué piece (Figure 19D). When you reach your starting point, secure the thread on the underside of the background with a backstitch.

FRENCH KNOT

A French knot is made by wrapping thread around a needle, then inserting the needle into the fabric or motif. Bring the needle and thread up from the bottom of the fabric to the point where you would like the knot to be positioned. Hold the thread taut and wrap it around the needle two or three times (Figure 20A). Insert the needle back through the top of the fabric very close to where it emerged (about $1/16$ inch away). Slip the wrapped thread down the length of the needle until it meets the fabric (Figure 20B). Push the needle through to the back,

FIGURE 19A

FIGURE 19B

FIGURE 19C

FIGURE 19D

and pull the thread through the loops and fabric until a small knot remains. Secure the stitch on the back of the fabric with a backstitch.

COUCHING

This is a decorative way to hold a long "line" of thread or other motif in place. Position the motif. Next, with either matching or contrasting thread, bring the needle up from the bottom of the fabric on one side of the motif, and go down again on the other side of the motif. Continue stitching over the motif at regular intervals (Figure 21).

BLANKET STITCH

The blanket stitch is thought of as a casual hand-finished detail. Work this stitch from right to left. Anchor your first stitch at the edge you are finishing. Point the needle toward you and insert it through the top of the fabric, about ¼ inch from the edge. Bring the point of the needle back up at the edge. With your thumb, guide the thread to form an L-shape on top of the fabric (Figure 22). Complete the stitch by pulling the needle through the fabric, making sure the "bottom" of the L-shape is looped under the needle. Continue, keeping your stitches evenly spaced and consistent in height.

FINISHING TECHNIQUES

In addition to pressing (see page 18), give your project or quilt a finished, crisp, and graphic appearance by using the following techniques.

PERFECT CORNERS

With a pencil, lightly mark the ¼-inch-wide seam allowances on the pieces you are machine-stitching. This makes it easier to pivot at corners as you machine-sew right angles. Following the pencil lines as you sew, "walk" (stitch using the hand-wheel) the needle to the penciled corner,

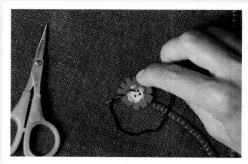

FIGURE 20A

FIGURE 20B

FIGURE 21

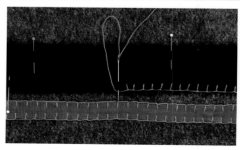

FIGURE 22

lower the needle to meet the corner, lift the foot, turn the fabric, lower the foot, and continue stitching along the next side.

TRIMMING AND POINT TURNING

Trimming refers to cutting away part of the seam allowance to reduce bulk, particularly important for corners and hems. Trim corners as shown, without cutting too close to the stitching (Figure 23). Turn the piece right side out. Insert a point turner into the corners and gently push out the corner points. Press flat, making sure the seam line rolls slightly to the wrong side.

CLIPPING

Clipping calls for cutting tiny slits into the seam allowance of curved edges so that the seam will lay flat when turned right side out. Make sure you don't clip into the stitches.

SQUARING UP

Even when you have been careful to cut accurately and stitch consistent seam allowances (see page 26), the size and shape of the block or piece may alter slightly during construction. To check your work, place the finished block or project on the cutting mat. Line up its edges, checking to see that 1) the lines are straight, and 2) the measurements are correct. Then, using a rotary cutter and an acrylic ruler, trim the block if needed (Figure 24). To make sure the sides of your quilt are straight and all corners are square, follow this same squaring up process prior to stitching on the binding. Since you may trim off your backstitching on seams when you square up, machine-stitch across any trimmed seams to keep them from coming apart.

FIGURE 23

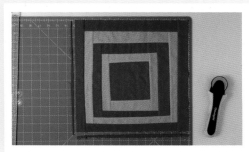

FIGURE 24

TWENTY PROJECTS

DIS-CARDS

These paper-and-fabric greetings are quick and fun to make. In fact, no sooner will you have finished one, then you'll want to make another. Use leftover scraps from other projects or slice off narrow lengths from your favorite vintage fabrics. Don't worry about frayed edges or having perfectly straight strips. The appeal of these cards is in their one-off variations of color and texture.

WHAT YOU NEED

A variety of colorful fabric scraps: enough to create several narrow 6-inch-long strips

One blank folded card: 4¼ inches by 5½ inches (or, a 5½-inch-by-8½ inch piece of card stock folded in half, then creased)

WHAT A CARD

You can make these cards in any size. Consider making tiny gift tags or give a set of gift-wrapped Dis-Cards along with a beautiful pen to a friend who likes to write personal notes.

(CONTINUED)

WHAT YOU DO

1 - To create the strips for the card Front, cut the fabric scraps in widths ranging from ¼ inch to 1½ inches. You'll need enough strips to cover the front surface of the card.

2 - Arrange the strips in a row, with right sides up, working from right to left, to create your design.

3 - When you are happy with the design, lay the open card right side up and position the first strip flush with the right-hand edge of the card. (The strip ends may extend beyond the top and bottom edges of the card, but you'll trim them later.) Stitch the strip to the card along the outer edge, backstitching at both ends to secure the stitches (Figure 1).

4 - Working right to left, position the next strip alongside the first, overlapping it slightly. Stitch through both strips (Figure 2). Add a third strip and continue until you reach the fold at the center of the card.

5 - When you reach the card's fold line, stitch through the fabric just short of the fold line (Figure 3). This will secure the left side of the outermost piece.

6 - Turn the card wrong side up and trim off any stray edges with a rotary cutter and ruler, being careful not to cut the card. Fold the card in half, and with wrong side up, trim the fabric along the fold, being careful not to cut into the card (Figure 4). Stitch along the top and bottom edges of the card.

7 - To "quilt" your card, topstitch it with straight lines or stitch horizontal and diagonal lines, allowing them to intersect. For a stitching design that will contrast with the inside of the card, use a contrasting thread. For a design that you want to blend with the inside, use thread in a color that matches your card. Snip thread ends close to card's surface.

Note: Change your needle after stitching card stock, as it can dull the point. Consider reserving needles to be used only for stitching cardboard or paper.

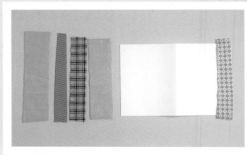

FIGURE 1

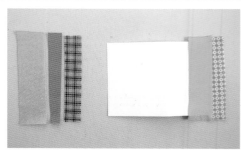

FIGURE 2

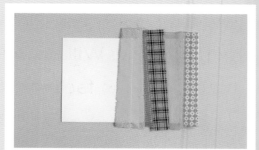

FIGURE 3

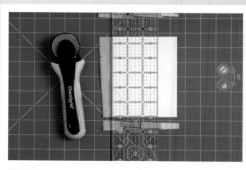

FIGURE 4

EYE WILL REVIVE EYE PILLOW

FINISHED SIZE: 4 INCHES BY 7½ INCHES

Take a minute—no, take five—to revive your eyes. This bright eye pillow is filled with a blend of flax seed, buckwheat hulls, and lavender. The weight of the flax seed and hulls provides gentle pressure when applied to tired eyes, and the fragrant lavender helps ease stress and tension. With the Eye Will Revive Eye Pillow on hand, you can face anything.

FILLING IT UP

To add the filling, make a funnel by coiling a square or rectangular piece of paper to create a cone. Snip the end (to about ¾ inch wide) and insert into the pillow's opening. Pour the filling through the funnel.

WHAT YOU NEED

Enlarge the "Eye Will Revive Eye Pillow" pattern on page 155 to 200 percent (see "Preparing the Pattern Pieces" on page 12).

FABRIC
FOR EYE PILLOW BACK AND LINING
Orange Blossom print: about ⅛ yard
Muslin or light-color cotton: about ⅛ yard

FOR EYE PILLOW FRONT
A total of about ¼ yard of cotton fabric scraps, pieces, or remnants, comprising the following (or your preferred) colors:

Aqua solid: about 8 inches by 5 inches for pattern pieces A, C, and E

Deep Aqua solid: about 2½ inches by 4 inches for B-Top and B-Bottom

No More Blue solid: about 2½ inches by 3½ inches for D-Top and D-Bottom

Orange Blossom print: about 2 inches square for B-Center

Sunny Side plaid: 1½-inch square for D-Center

OTHER MATERIALS
Flax seed: 1 cup
Buckwheat hulls: ⅓ cup
Lavender: 1 tablespoon

(CONTINUED)

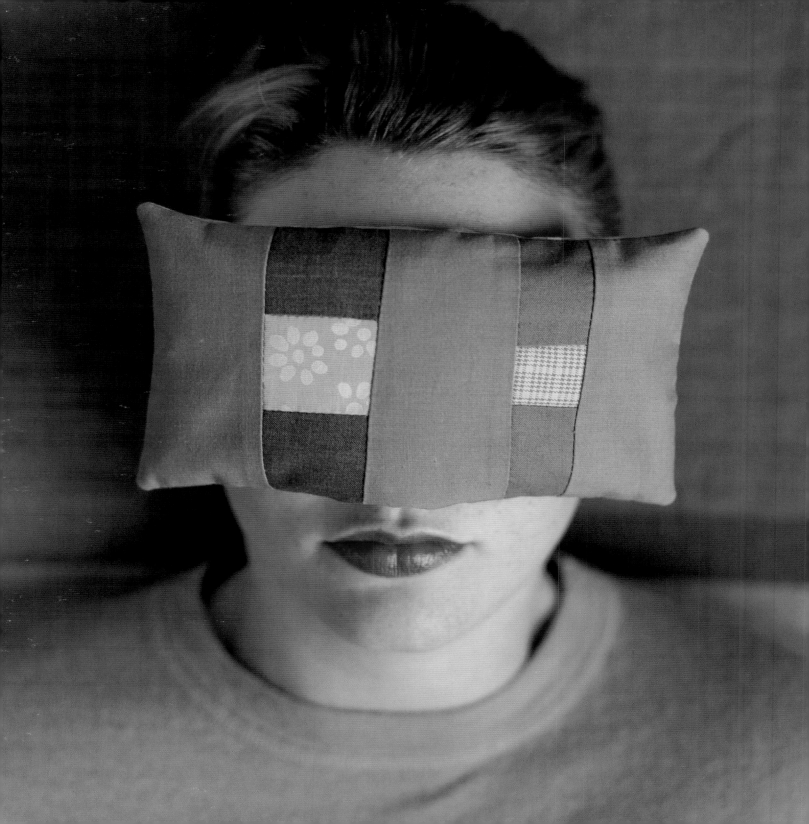

WHAT YOU DO

1 - From the Orange Blossom fabric, cut a 4½-inch-by-8-inch rectangle for the Eye Pillow Back. From the muslin, cut two 4½-inch-by-8-inch rectangles for the Lining pieces. Set them aside.

2 - Referring to "Laying Out and Cutting" on page 13, lay out and pin the enlarged pattern pieces to the right sides of the fabrics. Cut the Eye Pillow Front pieces and arrange them in the "Ready-Set-Sew" position (see page 14).

3 - First stitch B-Top to B-Center and B-Bottom to B-Center. Return the completed B piece to Ready-Set-Sew position. Repeat with the D pieces.

4 - Stitch together the Eye Pillow Front pieces, using the "String-Piecing Method" on page 16. Don't forget to use the "Compass Pin" (see page 15)!

5 - Center one Lining piece on the wrong side of the Eye Pillow Front, and machine-baste around the perimeter, ⅛ inch from the edge. Center the other Lining piece on the wrong side of the Eye Pillow Back, and machine-baste around the perimeter, ⅛ inch from the edge.

6 - With right sides together, lay the Eye Pillow Front on the Eye Pillow Back, aligning the edges and pinning as necessary. Leaving a 1½-inch-wide opening on one of the short sides (for turning and filling), stitch around the perimeter, pivoting at the corners (see "Perfect Corners" on page 28). Backstitch at the beginning and end of the seam to secure the stitches. Trim the corners.

7 - Turn the Eye Pillow right side out through the opening. Use a point turner to push out the corners (see "Trimming and Point Turning" on page 29). Press flat.

8 - Mix the flax seed, buckwheat hulls, and lavender toegther in a bowl or cup. Fill the pillow with the mixture (see "Filling It Up" on page 35).

9 - Use a slip stitch (see page 27) to close the seam opening, or stitch by machine close to the edge of the folds.

AN OPEN BOOK

An open book speaks volumes when filled with your memories and ideas. Make a journal and give the gift of potential to a friend who has always wanted to write, or make a multi-use book with photos, blank pages, and drawings commemorating a special event. After you've created the cover, take it (along with the interior pages) to a good local print shop. For a few dollars they'll cut the paper to size and wire-bind the book.

WHAT YOU NEED

TO MAKE THE VERTICAL FORMAT BOOK

FABRIC

A total of about ⅛ yard of cotton fabric pieces, scraps, or remnants, comprising the following (or your preferred) colors:

Colorful graphic print: about 4½ inches by 7½ inches for the Front Cover

Black solid: about 2½ inches by 7½ inches for the Spine Accent

OTHER MATERIALS

Medium-weight card stock: two 5½-inch-by-7-inch pieces for the Front and Back Covers

5½-inch-by-7-inch paper: approximately fifty sheets for the Interior Pages (see "What's Inside?" on this page)

Clear-drying fabric glue

WHAT'S INSIDE?

Paper arts or craft supply stores are good sources for a variety of fine papers, but you can also use paper from an office supply store. The number of sheets of paper you select for the Interior Pages depends on the paper's thickness. A good rule of thumb is to create a stack of Interior Pages about ½ inch thick. Note that one 8½-inch-by-11-inch sheet of paper will yield two pages, once trimmed. If you're making a photo album, it's a good idea to use fewer pages than you would for a journal, as the addition of photographs will increase the album's thickness.

(CONTINUED)

WHAT YOU DO

1 - Position the Front Cover fabric, right side up, on top of one of the card stock rectangles, allowing the fabric to extend ¼ inch beyond the top, bottom, and right edges of the card stock. Stitch the left side of the fabric to the card stock about 1 inch from the card stock edge, leaving enough room for holes to be drilled or punched later; backstitch at the beginning and end of the stitched line to secure the stitches (Figure 1).

2 - With right sides together, lay the Spine Accent on top of the Front Cover fabric. Align the edge of the Spine Accent with the left edge of the Front Cover fabric. Stitch through all the layers with a ¼-inch-wide seam allowance, backstitching at the beginning and end of the seam to secure the stitches (Figure 2).

3 - Fold back the Spine Accent, and edgestitch along the seam to keep the fold flat.

4 - Turn over the Front Cover, card stock facing up, and stitch around the perimeter, a scant ⅛ inch from the edge (Figure 3). As you sew, keep the fabric taut to ensure the Front Cover fabric will lay smooth and flat.

5 - With a rotary cutter and an acrylic ruler, trim any excess fabric, making certain not to cut into the card stock (Figure 4). To prevent the fabric cover from fraying, dab clear-drying fabric glue on all the cut edges.

6 - To embellish the Front Cover, machine-stitch a design (straight, zigzagged, or diagonal lines) in contrasting thread. Snip the thread ends close to the cover's surface.

7 - Take your Front and Back Covers and Interior Pages to a local print shop to have them cut the Interior Pages to size. With the completed stack of Interior Pages and the Covers, the shop staff can assist you in selecting the right size of wire binding and can bind the entire book together for you.

Note: Change your needle after stitching card stock, as it can dull the point. Consider reserving needles to be used only for stitching cardboard or paper.

FIGURE 1

FIGURE 2

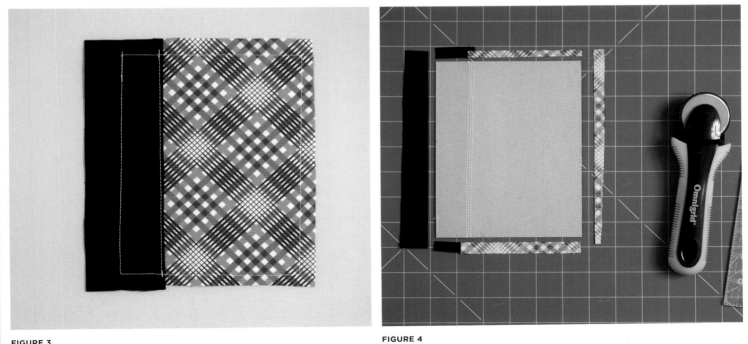

FIGURE 3

FIGURE 4

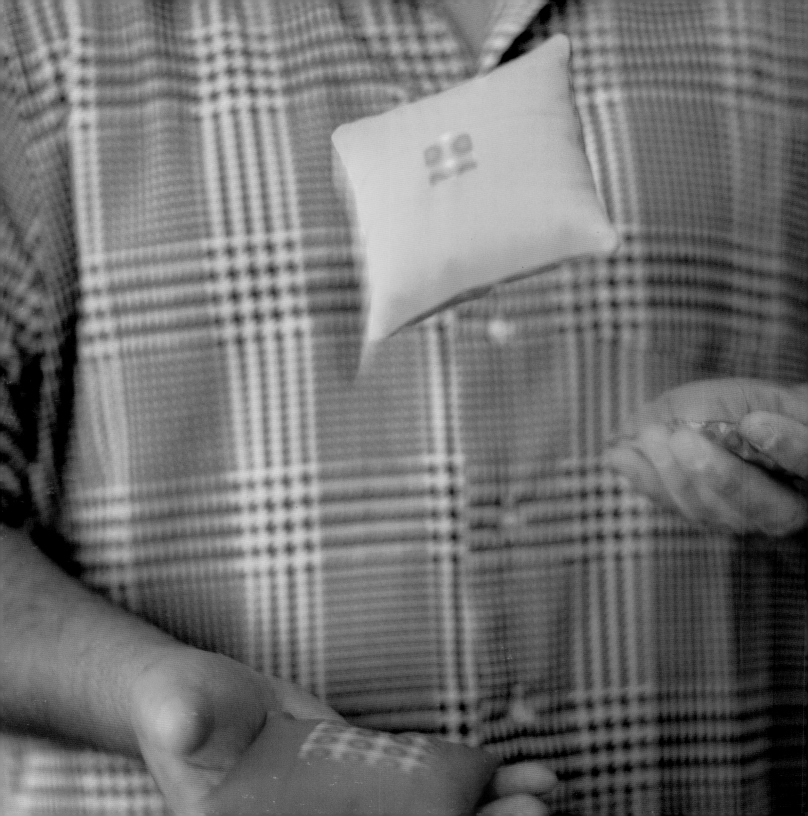

CARES IN THE AIR JUGGLING BLOCKS

MAKES THREE JUGGLING BLOCKS · FINISHED SIZE: 4 INCHES BY 4 INCHES

Toss your cares in the air—and then run like hell! If only it were as easy to escape our worries as it is to make these lentil-filled amusements. Not only is juggling a fun way to de-stress and relax, but you also burn calories, firm your upper arms, and impress your co-workers. Why not make them for all the harried, overworked, perfection-seeking, multi-tasking people in your life?

WHAT YOU NEED

Enlarge the "Cares in the Air Juggling Blocks" pattern on page 156 to 200 percent (see "Preparing the Pattern Pieces" on page 12).

FABRIC
FOR THE BACKS AND LININGS

Watermelon print: ⅛ yard for the Block Backs

Muslin or light-colored cotton: ⅛ yard for the Linings

FOR THE FRONTS
A total of ¼ yard of cotton fabric scraps, pieces, or remnants, comprising the following (or your preferred) colors:

Watermelon print: about 5-inch-by-5-inch square for Centers

Cherry solid: about 5-inch-by-6-inch rectangle for Block 1 Front

Tangerine solid: about 5-inch-by-7-inch rectangle for Block 2 Front

Pumpkin solid: about 5-inch-by-6½-inch rectangle for Block 3 Front

OTHER MATERIALS
Dried lentils: about one 16-ounce bag, measured into three ⅔-cup portions for each block

(CONTINUED)

WHAT YOU DO

1 - From the Watermelon print, cut three 4½-inch-by-4½-inch squares for the Block Backs. From the muslin, cut six 4½-inch-by-4½-inch squares for the Linings. Set them aside.

2 - Referring to "Laying Out and Cutting" on page 13, lay out and pin the enlarged pattern pieces to the right sides of the fabrics. Cut out the Block Front pieces for Blocks 1, 2, and 3. Arrange the pieces for each block in the "Ready-Set-Sew" position (see page 14).

3 - Using the "Compass Pin" (see page 15) and referring to the "Modified–Log Cabin Method" on page 15, assemble the Block Fronts. Keep in mind that these blocks have only one "frame" each, so you will only need to refer to Steps 1, 2, and 3 of the Modified–Log Cabin Method.

4 - Center the Lining on the wrong side of Block 1 Front, and machine-baste around the perimeter, ⅛ inch from the edge. Center the Lining on the wrong side of a Block Back, and machine-baste around the perimeter, ⅛ inch from the edge. Repeat for Blocks 2 and 3.

5 - With right sides together, lay the Block 1 Front on a Block Back, aligning the edges, and pin. Leaving a 1½-inch-wide opening at the center bottom (for turning), stitch around the perimeter of the square, pivoting at the corners (see "Perfect Corners" on page 28). Backstitch at the beginning and end of each seam to secure the stitches. Trim the corners. Repeat for Blocks 2 and 3.

6 - Turn the blocks right side out through the opening. Use a point turner to push out the corners (see "Trimming and Point Turning" on page 29). Press flat. Fill with lentils (see "Filling It Up" on page 35). Use the slip stitch (see page 27) to close the seam opening, or stitch by machine, close to the edge of the folds.

FRAME OF MINE

FINISHED SIZE: 5 INCHES BY 7 INCHES

Transform a store-bought clip frame into a one-of-a-kind setting for your favorite photograph. Choose fabrics and colors that enhance the image, or make it more personal by using fabric scraps from clothing or other items that you associate with the person in your photograph. If you plan to travel, consider purchasing an inexpensive bandanna, kitschy souvenir dishtowel, or brightly colored scarf to use for fabric to back a picture of the place you visited. Keep in mind that the photograph should be smaller than the frame itself.

WHAT YOU NEED

Enlarge the "Frame of Mine" pattern on page 155 to 200 percent (see "Preparing the Pattern Pieces" on page 12).

FABRIC

A total of about ⅛ yard of cotton fabric pieces, scraps, or remnants, comprising the following (or your preferred) colors:

Red solid: about 5 inches by 7 inches for A-Top Right and C-Bottom Right pieces

Tangerine plaid: about 2½ inches by 6 inches for A-Bottom

Orange solid: about 4½ inches by 5 inches for A-Top Left and C-Top pieces

Orange plaid: about 1½ inches by 3 inches for C-Bottom Left

Orange print: about 2½ inches by 6 inches for B and C-Center

OTHER MATERIALS
5-inch-by-7-inch clip frame

(CONTINUED)

WHAT YOU DO

1 - Referring to "Laying Out and Cutting" on page 13, lay out the enlarged pattern pieces on the right sides of the fabrics, and pin. Cut out all of the pieces. Arrange in the "Ready-Set-Sew" position (see page 14).

2 - Referring to the "String-Piecing Method" on page 16, stitch the pieces together, pressing the seams *open* as you work (so the seams lay flat under your photo). Stitch in the following order: Stitch A-Top Left to A-Top Right. Then, stitch the pieced A-Top to A-Bottom. Next, stitch C-Bottom Left to C-Bottom Right. Then, stitch the pieced C-Bottom to C-Center. Stitch C-Center to C-Top. Finally, stitch A to B, and B to C.

3 - Square up the patchwork-pieced background (see "Squaring Up" on page 29) to 5 inches by 7 inches. A good way to determine where to trim the stitched background piece is to move the frame's glass around the top of the fabric until you like what you see beneath the glass (Figure 1).

4 - Assemble the frame, positioning the fabric block right side up on top of the frame's backing board, with the edges aligned. Next, position your photo in the center of the fabric block, and place the glass on top. Clip the glass and frame backing board together.

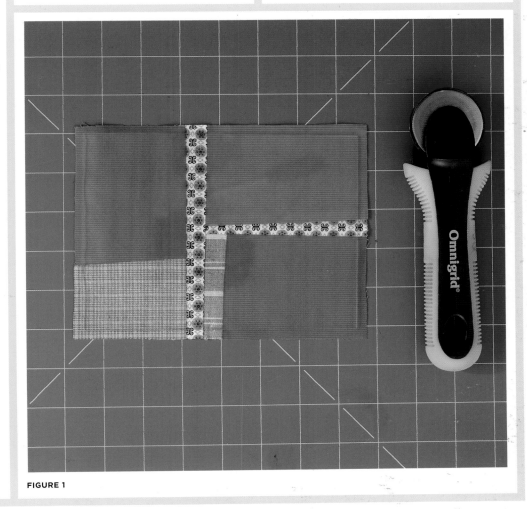

FIGURE 1

ZIGZAG BAG

FINISHED SIZE: 11 INCHES BY 13 INCHES

Yes, you can take it with you—and you probably should! This great-looking vinyl bag is the perfect size for all your needs. Slip in your flip-flops, files, and phone, then sneak off to the beach for the afternoon. The vinyl gives this bag body and makes it easy to clean. The tape measure handles are a sure-fire conversation starter and provide a useful tool (especially in situations where size does matter).

WHAT YOU NEED
FABRIC
A total of about ¾ yard of vinyl pieces or remnants, comprising the following (or your preferred) colors:

Note: This is enough yardage to make the "Zigzag Zip" (see page 53) too.

Turquoise: about ⅜ yard for the Bag Base

Mahogany: about ⅓ yard for the Bag Bottom

OTHER MATERIALS AND TOOLS
Vinyl tape measure: 60 inches long (or an equal substitute of your choice)

A Teflon foot for your sewing machine (optional: makes it easy to sew vinyl)

PUTTING THE ZIGZAG ON YOUR BAG
Improvise as you machine-quilt the zigzags so they don't end up looking too "perfect." Vary the depth of the points and the stitch angles, and don't bother trying to keep your stitch lines perfectly straight.

(CONTINUED)

WHAT YOU DO

1 - From the Turquoise vinyl, cut a 12-inch-by-28-inch rectangle for the Bag Base. Set aside. From the Mahogany, cut a 12-inch-by-10-inch rectangle for the Bag Bottom. Center the Bottom rectangle on the Base rectangle, using the grid on your cutting mat as a guide. Tape the edges of the Bottom rectangle to the Base (Figure 1).

2 - Secure the Bottom to the Base as follows in preparation for machine-quilting: With your sewing machine set to 10 stitches per inch, stitch along the outer edges of the Bottom. With chalk and your acrylic ruler, lightly mark the centerline on the Bottom (Figure 2). Then stitch along the chalk line through both layers. Remove the tape, and stitch both sides of the Bottom close to the edges (Figure 3).

3 - Create the machine-quilting by stitching tall zigzags across the Bag Bottom. The points of the zigzags are about 1½ inches apart. Beginning at one corner of the Bag Bottom along the outer edge, stitch across the Bottom at a slight angle, stopping with needle down, about 1 inch to 1½ inches from the outer edge and ¼ inch to 1 inch into the Bag Base area. With the needle down, pivot the vinyl 180 degrees. Now stitch back across at a slight angle (aim to make your next point end about 1 inch to 1½ inches from where you began stitching). Be sure to stop, with the needle down, about ¼ to 1 inch into the Base area, and pivot the Bag with the needle down. Continue stitching until you have covered the Bag Bottom with zigzags (Figure 4).

4 - When you reach the opposite outer edge of the Bag Bottom, start again, this time stitching a second set of tall zigzags in between the first (Figure 5).

5 - Right sides together, fold the Bag Base in half, and stitch the side seams with a ½-inch-wide seam allowance. Trim the corners and the seam allowance at the upper edges of the Bag. Turn the Bag right side out. (See "Trimming and Point Turning" on page 29, but skip the pressing!)

6 - Fold down a 1-inch-wide hem along the top edge. Stitch in place, close to the raw edge.

7 - Trim off the metal ends of the tape measure, and cut it into two 26-inch lengths. Position each of the handle ends on the inside of the Bag, 2 inches inside the side seams and 1 inch below the top edge of Bag. Stitch in place, zigzagging across the tape ends (Figure 6).

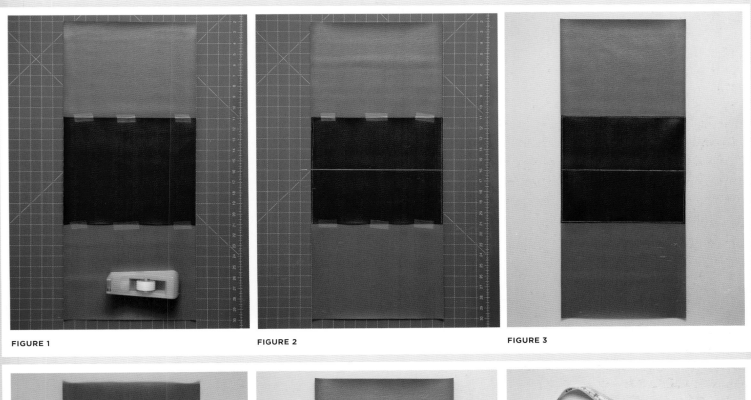

FIGURE 1

FIGURE 2

FIGURE 3

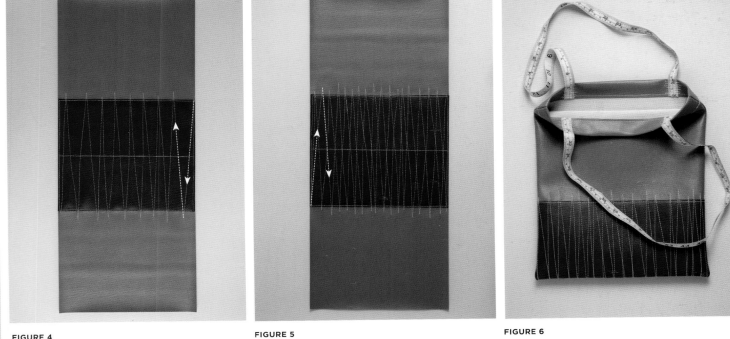

FIGURE 4

FIGURE 5

FIGURE 6

ZIGZAG ZIP

FINISHED SIZE: 5 INCHES BY 6 INCHES

Let's see. . .in an hour or less you can: 1) clean the bathroom, 2) balance your checkbook, or 3) whip up the Zigzag Zip. It's a snappy little purse perfect for those times when you're traveling light, and it's just big enough to hold money, gum, lip balm, and keys. Slip the Zip into your pocket and go!

WHAT YOU NEED

FABRIC

A total of less than ¼ yard of pieces or remnants of vinyl, comprising the following (or your preferred) colors:

Mahogany: 7½-inch-by-13-inch piece for the Purse

Turquoise: 6½-inch-by-3-inch piece for the Accents

OTHER MATERIALS AND TOOLS

A Teflon foot for your sewing machine (optional: makes it easy to sew vinyl)

6-inch-long zipper: if you wish, color-coordinate the zipper to match your "Zigzag Bag" tape-measure handles (see page 49)

(CONTINUED)

WHAT YOU DO

1 - From the Mahogany, cut two 6-inch-by-7-inch rectangles. Set aside. From the Turquoise, cut two Accent Strips that measure approximately 6 inches by 1¼ inches. Cut these freehand to give them a bit of personality.

2 - Position one Accent Strip about 2 inches in from one edge of one Purse rectangle. To hold it in place, machine-baste the strip at both ends. Trim the ends of the strips to the size of the Purse (Figure 1).

3 - With your sewing machine stitch-length set to 10 stitches per inch, stitch through the Accent Strip in a zigzag pattern as follows: Beginning at one side of the Purse, stitch at a slight angle through the Accent Strip, into the Purse area about ¼ to ½ inches, and stop with needle down. Pivot the vinyl 180 degrees and stitch back, ending about ½ inch from where you started. Vary the stitch angle to make your zigzag points closer together or farther apart. Repeat until you have zigzag-stitched the entire Accent Strip. See "Putting the Zigzag on Your Bag" on page 49 for more on making the zigzag stitching.

4 - Repeat Steps 2 and 3 for the other side of the Purse.

5 - Position the Purse rectangles, right side up and long edges facing each other. Make sure the Accent Strips are aligned. Fold under ½ inch on each of the long Purse sides that face each other. Edgestitch along the folds (Figure 2). (Do not pin, as this will leave holes in the vinyl!)

6 - With right sides up, lay the folded edges of the Purse over the zipper tape. The zipper should be zipped closed. Position so that the zipper pull is a little more than ½ inch from the Purse side edge. Stitch along the folds close to the edge, through all the layers (Figure 3).

7 - Unzip the zipper nearly all the way. With right sides together, stitch the remaining three sides of the Purse using a ½-inch-wide seam allowance, pivoting at corners. Trim the corners (see page 29), and snip off the ends of zipper (Figure 4). Turn the Purse right side out.

FIGURE 1

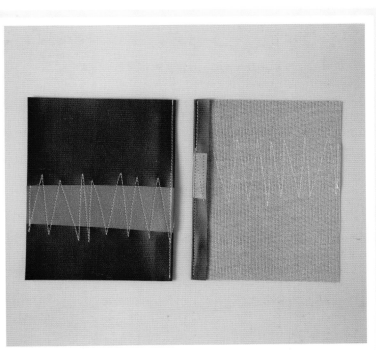

FIGURE 2

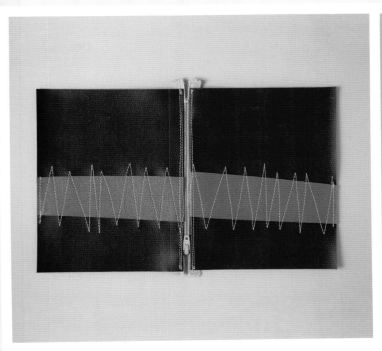

FIGURE 3

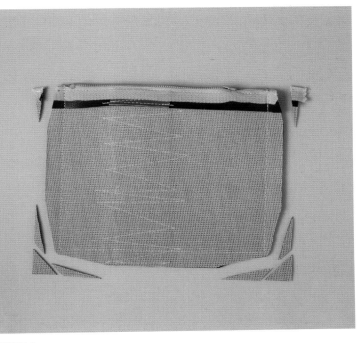

FIGURE 4

SCRAP WRAP

FINISHED SIZE: 63 INCHES BY 7 INCHES

Combine the woven texture of wool suiting with the soft sheen of colorful silk in this elegant accessory. The Scrap Wrap is made using the "Foundation-Piecing Method" on page 17 and is just right for anyone who likes to make up things as they go along. The scarf shown here includes vintage kimono accents (see "Resources" on page 171), but you can experiment with any combination of heavy-textured and fine-weave fabrics. Make the coordinating "A Muff Is a Muff" on page 61 to complete your cool-weather ensemble.

WHAT YOU NEED

FABRIC

A total of about ⅞ yard of fabric, comprising wool, silk, or cotton fabric pieces or remnants, in the following (or your preferred) colors:

Brown/Black herringbone: ¼ yard for the Scarf Top

Brown/Tan bouclé: ¼ yard for the Scarf Top

Brown/Burgundy houndstooth check: ¼ yard for the Scarf Top

Red/Pink silk, wool, or cotton prints: about ⅛ yard total, in a variety of prints for the Accent Stripes

Muslin: ½ yard for the Foundation

Powder Pink wool, flannel, or satin: ½ yard for the Lining

(CONTINUED)

WHAT YOU DO

1 - From the three brown Scarf Top fabrics, cut several strips selvage to selvage (see page 13) in varying widths ranging from 2 to 4 inches. Put your acrylic ruler away for this step. The idea is to cut freeform strips that are somewhat, but not perfectly, straight. Set the strips aside.

2 - From the Red/Pink Accent Stripe fabrics, cut three 15½-inch-long strips and six 8½-inch-long strips, all of varying widths ranging from 1 to 1¼ inch. Set aside.

3 - From the Foundation fabric, cut one 36½-by-8½-inch rectangle and two 15½-by-8½-inch rectangles. Set aside.

4 - From the Lining fabric, cut two 32½-inch-by-8 inch rectangles.

5 - Right sides together, with a ½-inch-wide seam allowance, stitch the Lining rectangles together end to end to make one long rectangle. Press the seam open. Set aside.

6 - Lay out the three Foundation rectangles on a flat surface, positioned so that the two shorter rectangles flank the long one. Arrange the Scarf Top strips and Accent Stripes on the Foundation rectangles. (Note that strips run lengthwise on the two outer rectangles and widthwise on the center one.) Alternate fabric textures, and position the wider strips next to the narrower ones. Stagger the Accent Stripes (Figures 1 and 2). Overlap the strip edges about ½ inch to allow for the seam allowance.

7 - When you are pleased with your design, remove the strips from the Foundation rectangles, keeping them in "Ready-Set-Sew" position (see page 14) (Figures 3, 4, and 5).

8 - Referring to the "Foundation-Piecing Method" on page 17 and working left to right, stitch all the strips to the Foundation. Press with an iron set to "Wool," with the steam setting on.

9 - Turn the Foundation piece over (strip side down) and square up your piece (see "Squaring Up" on page 29) to 8 inches by 15 inches. Machine-baste all four edges of the rectangle, ⅛ inch from the edge (Figure 6). Repeat with the other short rectangle.

10 - Referring to the Foundation-Piecing Method and working left to right, stitch the strips to the long rectangle. After all the strips have been stitched, turn the rectangle over (strip side down) and square up to 8 inches by 36 inches. Machine-baste all four edges of the rectangle after squaring up, ⅛ inch from the edge.

11 - Right sides together, stitch one short rectangle to either end of the longer rectangle, with a ½-inch-wide seam allowance. Press the seams open.

12 - With right sides together and the edges aligned, stitch the Lining to the front with a ½-inch-wide seam allowance, leaving a 7-inch-wide opening in the center of one long side for turning. Press. Trim the corners, and then turn the wrap right side out (Figure 7). Use a point turner to push out the corners (see "Trimming and Point Turning" on page 29). Press flat. Use the slip stitch (see page 27) to close the opening.

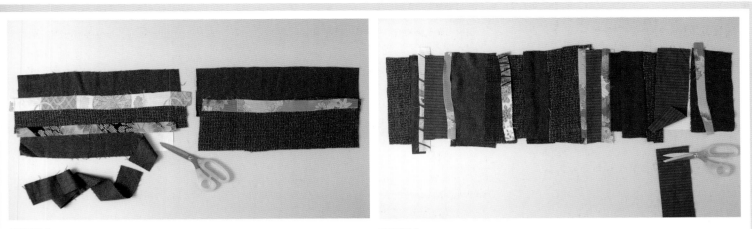

FIGURE 1

FIGURE 2

FIGURE 3

FIGURE 4

FIGURE 5

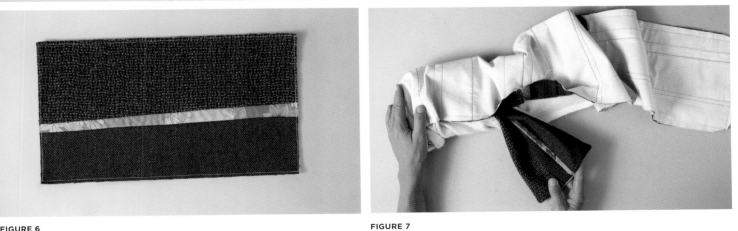

FIGURE 6

FIGURE 7

A MUFF IS A MUFF

FINISHED SIZE: 10 INCHES BY 9 INCHES

No more crying over a lost glove! The muff is a smart accessory whose time has come again. Dialing your phone, finding your keys in the bottom of your bag, paying for purchases—all are a snap with no time lost fumbling to remove your gloves. Make this beautiful winter hand-warmer using wool and silk, a juxtaposition of textures as pleasing to the hands as it is to the eyes. After a long day of working, shopping, or skating, slip the soft muff under your head and take a snooze as the bus or train shuttles you home.

WHAT YOU NEED

FABRIC

A total of about ½ yard of wool, silk, and cotton fabric pieces or remnants, comprising the following (or your preferred) colors:

Brown/Black herringbone: ⅛ yard for the Muff Front

Brown/Tan bouclé: ⅛ yard for the Muff Front

Brown/Burgundy houndstooth check: ⅛ yard for the Muff Front

Red/Pink silk, wool, or cotton prints: ⅛ yard total in a variety of prints for the Accent Stripes

Powder Pink wool, flannel, or satin: ⅓ yard for the Lining

Muslin: ½ yard for the Foundation

OTHER MATERIALS

High-loft polyester batting: ½ yard

(CONTINUED)

WHAT YOU DO

1 - From the three brown Muff Front fabrics, cut several strips selvage to selvage (see page 13) in varying widths ranging from $1\frac{1}{2}$ to $4\frac{1}{2}$ inches. Put your acrylic ruler away for this step. The idea is to cut free-form strips that are somewhat, but not perfectly, straight.

2 - From the Red/Pink prints, cut two 22-inch strips in varying widths, ranging from 1 to $1\frac{1}{4}$ inches for the Accent Stripes. Set them aside.

3 - From the Lining fabric, cut one 21-inch-by-$9\frac{1}{2}$-inch rectangle. Set aside. From the batting, cut two 20-inch-by-10-inch rectangles. Set them aside. From the Foundation fabric, cut one 22-inch-by-14-inch rectangle.

4 - Arrange the Muff Front strips and Accent Stripes lengthwise on the Foundation rectangle. Alternate fabric textures, and position the wider strips next to the narrower ones. Stagger the Accent Stripes (Figure 1). Overlap the strip edges about $\frac{1}{2}$ inch to allow for the seam allowances.

5 - When you are pleased with your design, remove the strips from the Foundation rectangle, keeping them in the "Ready-Set-Sew" position (see page 14).

6 - Referring to the "Foundation-Piecing Method" on page 17 and working left to right, stitch all the strips to the Foundation rectangle. Press with an iron with the steam feature on and set to "Wool."

7 - Turn the piece over (strip side down) and square up the piece (see "Squaring Up" on page 29) to 21 inches by 13 inches. Machine-baste all four edges of the Muff Front, $\frac{1}{8}$ inch from the edge.

8 - With right sides together, fold the Muff Front in half, end to end, and stitch the ends together with a $\frac{1}{2}$-inch-wide seam allowance. You will now have a tube that measures $10\frac{1}{2}$ by 13 inches. Press the seam open.

9 - Mark both ends of the Muff Front in quarters by folding the tube in half lengthwise, then in half again. Use the fold lines as a guide for chalk marks (Figure 2).

10 - With right sides together, fold the Lining in half, end to end, and stitch with a $\frac{1}{2}$-inch-wide seam allowance. You will now have a tube that measures $10\frac{1}{2}$ by $9\frac{1}{2}$ inches. Mark each end in quarters as in Step 9. Press the seam open. Turn the Lining right side out.

11 - Slip the Lining tube inside the Muff Front Tube (right sides together), and pin the raw edges together on one end, aligning seams and chalk marks. With a $\frac{1}{2}$-inch-wide seam allowance, stitch along the pinned edge (Figure 3). Press the seam flat, then turn out the Muff Lining and press the seam allowance toward the lining (Figure 4).

12 - Machine-baste the open ends of the Muff Front and Lining a scant (see page 23) $\frac{1}{2}$ inch from the edge. Turn $\frac{1}{2}$ inch of the free end of the Lining toward the wrong side, and press to hold it in place (Figure 5).

13 - Center the two layers of batting on the Muff Front. Wrap the loose ends of the inside layer around the muff until they meet at the Front seam allowance. Whipstitch (see page 27) the edges of the batting together to form a tube (Figure 6). Repeat with the outside layer of batting. Your Muff Front will be compressed inside the batting tube (Figure 7).

14 - Turn the Lining, right side out, over the batting. Keeping the batting centered, fold the free end of the Muff Front toward the Lining. Pin the Lining's folded edge to the right side of the Muff Front along the machine basting, seams and chalk marks aligned (Figure 8). Use the slip stitch (see page 27) to secure the Lining to the Muff (Figure 9). Turn the Muff right side out.

FIGURE 1

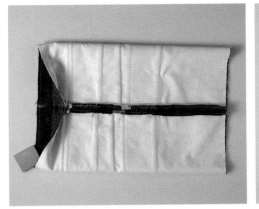

FIGURE 2

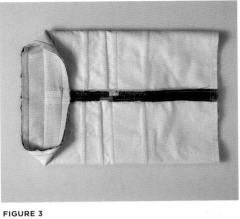

FIGURE 3

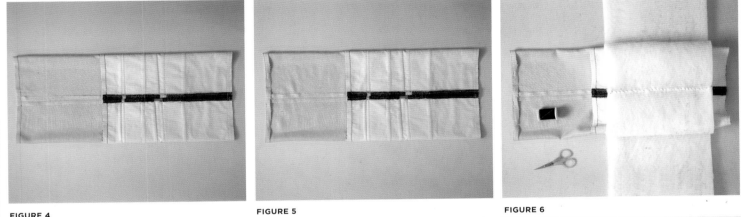

FIGURE 4

FIGURE 5

FIGURE 6

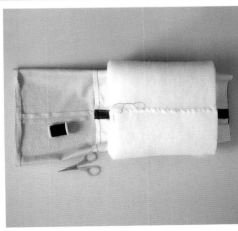

FIGURE 7

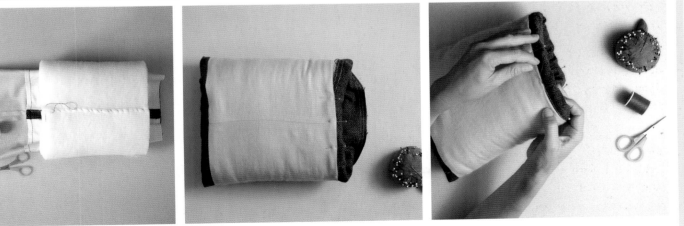

FIGURE 8

FIGURE 9

MIX-IT-UP COCKTAIL COASTERS

MAKES SIX COASTERS - FINISHED SIZE: 4 INCHES BY 4 INCHES

Stitched up in colors reminiscent of your favorite cocktails—frozen margaritas, Blue Lagoons, mint juleps, and martinis with a twist—a set of these coasters makes a perfect gift. Give them away along with a set of coordinating swizzle sticks or glasses. Select six fabrics in shades of lemon and lime, then layer them, three to a pile, and cut out the pattern pieces. After that, shuffle the pieces to mix up the colors and see what you get!

WHAT YOU NEED

Enlarge the "Mix-It-Up Cocktail Coasters" pattern on page 157 to 200 percent (see "Preparing the Pattern Pieces" on page 12).

FABRIC AND OTHER MATERIALS
FOR THE COASTER BACKS
Lime Green: about ⅛ yard
Cotton batting: about ⅛ yard

FOR THE COASTER FRONTS
A total of about ¼ yard of cotton fabric pieces, scraps, or remnants, comprising the following (or your favorite) colors, each cut into 5-inch-by-8-inch rectangles:

Lemon Yellow plaid
Cocktail Shaker Silver geometric print
Curaçao Blue solid
Crème de Menthe Green solid
Olive Green solid
Lime Green solid

(CONTINUED)

WHAT YOU DO

1 - From the Lime Green fabric, cut six 4½-inch-by-4½-inch squares for the Coaster Backs. From the cotton batting, cut six 4½-inch-by-4½-inch squares for the Coaster padding. Set aside.

2 - Stack three of the Coaster Front fabric rectangles (any three of the six colors), right sides up, edges aligned. Referring to "Laying Out and Cutting" on page 13, lay out the enlarged pattern pieces on top of the stack, pinning through all the layers (Figure 1). Cut out all the pieces. Repeat with the remaining three Coaster Front fabric rectangles.

3 - Position each color separately in "Ready-Set-Sew" (see page 14) (Figure 2).

4 - Give each coaster a unique color combination by shuffling the pieces until each block has a mix of fabrics and colors. You can work systematically, moving all of the A pieces around first, for instance, then moving the B pieces, and so on. Or you can improvise, swapping out colors until you're pleased with the results (Figures 3, 4, and 5). Just remember to keep the pieces in the Ready-Set-Sew position as you work!

5 - Referring to the "String-Piecing Method" (see page 16), stitch all Coaster Front pieces together, aligning the points where the seam lines intersect on each piece (Figure 6). Press the seam allowances of the A and F pieces toward their outside edges. The rest of the seam allowances should be pressed toward the darker fabric. Square up (see page 29) each Coaster Front, then machine-baste around the perimeter of each, ⅛ inch from the edge.

6 - Center one square of batting on the wrong side of each of the Coaster Backs, and machine-baste around the perimeter of each one, ⅛ inch from the edge.

7 - With right sides together, lay the Coaster Fronts on the Coaster Backs, aligning the edges and pinning if necessary. Leaving a 1¼-inch-wide opening at the center bottom for turning, stitch around the perimeter of the square, pivoting at corners (see "Perfect Corners" on page 28). Backstitch at the beginning and end of the seam to secure the stitches. Trim corners.

8 - Turn each Coaster right side out through the opening. Use a point turner to push out the corners (see "Trimming and Point Turning" on page 29). Press flat. Use the slip stitch (see page 27) to close the opening, or stitch by machine, close to the edge of the folds.

9 - Referring to the "Hand-Quilting Stitch" on page 21, stitch-in-the-ditch (see page 20). If you'd prefer, machine-quilt the coasters. See "Machine-Quilting" on page 23.

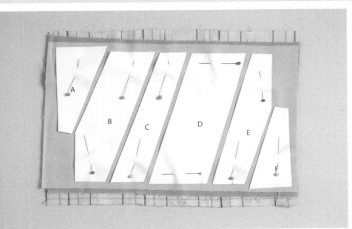

FIGURE 1

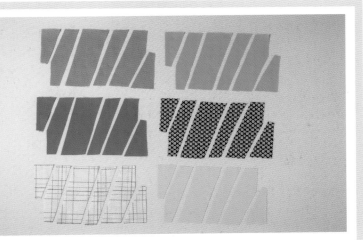

FIGURE 2

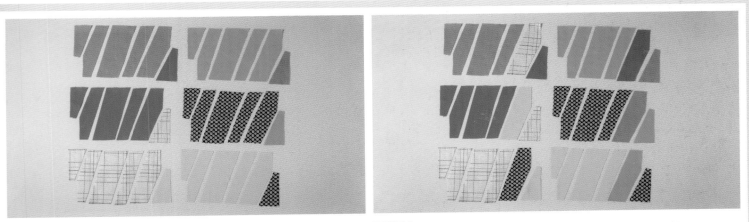

FIGURE 3

FIGURE 4

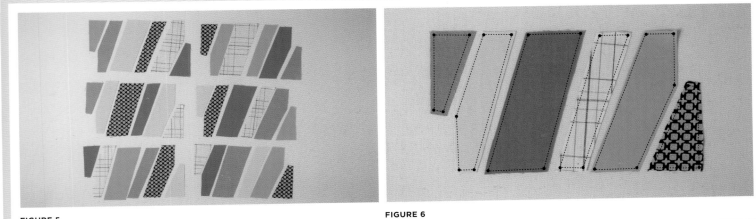

FIGURE 5

FIGURE 6

SHIMMY, SHAKE & BAKE APRON

FINISHED SIZE: 22½ INCHES BY 28 INCHES

Whoa! Suddenly the oven is *not* the hottest thing in the kitchen! This apron is fun to make, and even more fun to wear. Shim, sham, shimmy all around the kitchen, and the pom-pom trim will swing right along with you. The multi-color block pocket is the perfect place to keep your recipe cards close at hand. Turn up the radio and bake up some action.

SIZE IT UP
The instructions here are for a women's size small/medium. If you want to make a different size, adjust the yardage accordingly.

WHAT YOU NEED
Enlarge the "Shimmy, Shake & Bake Apron" pattern on page 158 to 200 percent (see "Preparing the Pattern Pieces" on page 12).

FABRIC AND OTHER MATERIALS
POCKET LINING
Muslin: ¼ yard

Non-woven, non-fusible, medium-weight interfacing: ¼ yard

POCKET FRONT
A total of about ½ yard of cotton fabric pieces, scraps, or remnants, comprising the following (or your preferred) colors:

Egg White solid: about 2½ inches by 4 inches for the A pieces

Food Coloring Blues: about 13 inches by 15 inches in total of four different blue fabrics for the Center and B pieces (we used one floral print, one calico, one "bubble" print, and one solid)

Hot Pepper Reds: about 12 inches by 15 inches total of two different red fabrics for C pieces (we used one solid and one print)

Unbleached cotton canvas: 1 yard for the Apron Front and Apron Ties

Oatmeal or white pom-pom trim: 1 yard

(CONTINUED)

WHAT YOU DO

MAKING THE POCKET

1 - From the muslin, cut a 9½-inch-by-9-inch piece. From the interfacing, cut a 9½-inch-by-9-inch piece. These pieces will be used to create the Pocket Lining. Set aside.

2 - Referring to "Laying Out and Cutting" on page 13, lay out and pin the enlarged pattern pieces to the right sides of the Pocket Front fabrics. Cut out and arrange all the pieces in the "Ready-Set-Sew" position (see page 14).

3 - With right sides together, stitch C-Left-1 to C-Left-2, and press. Using a "Compass Pin" (see page 15) and referring to the "Modified–Log Cabin Method" on page 15, stitch all the Pocket pieces together.

4 - Square up the Pocket Front to 9½ inches by 9 inches (see "Squaring Up" on page 29), then machine-baste around the perimeter of the Pocket Front, ⅛ inch from the edge.

5 - With *wrong* sides together, center the interfacing on top of the Lining. Machine-baste around the perimeter, ⅛ inch from the edge. With the interfacing side up, place the muslin Lining on the right side of the Pocket Front, aligning the edges and pinning, if necessary.

6 - Leaving a 2-inch-wide opening at the center bottom of the Pocket for turning, stitch around the perimeter of the square through all layers, pivoting at corners (see "Perfect Corners" on page 28). Backstitch at the beginning and end of the seam to secure the stitches. Trim the corners.

7 - Turn the Pocket right side out through the opening. Use a point turner to push out the corners (see "Trimming and Point Turning" on page 29). Press flat. Edgestitch (see page 26) to close the opening.

MAKING THE TIES

1 - From the canvas, cut two 36-inch-by-1¾-inch strips for the Ties.

2 - Fold under ½ inch at one short end of each Tie. Press. Trim the corners of the folded edge (Figure 1A).

3 - Fold the long edges of each Tie inward so they meet in the center, and press (Figure 1B).

4 - Next, fold the Tie in half lengthwise (Figure 1C). Press. Stitch along the open length and across the finished end of the Tie. Repeat for the second Tie. Set aside.

MAKING THE APRON

1 - From the canvas, cut one 30-inch-by-25-inch rectangle for the Apron Front. If you like, adjust the width to customize the Apron size.

2 - With the Apron Front positioned horizontally, double-turn (see page 26) a ½-inch-wide hem on each short side (Figure 2).

3 - Center the pom-pom trim on the right side of the Apron along the bottom edge, pom-poms toward the top of the Apron and the trim's tape just covering the raw edge. Pin. Cut the ends of tape so that ½ inch extends beyond each side of the Apron (Figure 3). Clip off any pom-poms from the tape ends.

4 - Fold the cut ends of the pom-pom trim to the back of the Apron, and pin (Figure 4). Edgestitch the pom-pom side of the trim to the Apron, backstitching at the beginning and end of the seam to secure the stitches.

5 - Turn up the bottom of the Apron toward the wrong side, ½ inch or the width of the trim tape, and pin (Figure 5). To finish the hem, stitch along the free edge of the trim tape through all the layers, backstitching to secure.

6 - Machine-stitch the raw ends of the Ties to the wrong side of the Apron at the top corners. Double-turn a ½-inch hem at the top edge of the Apron, and stitch (Figure 6). Backstitch across the Ties at the corners to reinforce the spot where the Ties join the Apron.

7 - Center the Pocket on the Apron, about 4 inches below the top edge of the Apron, and pin. Topstitch (see page 26) close to the edge of the Pocket sides and bottom to the Apron, and reinforce top corners with a reverse-triangle stitch (Figure 7).

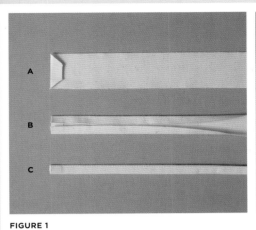

FIGURE 1

FIGURE 2

FIGURE 3

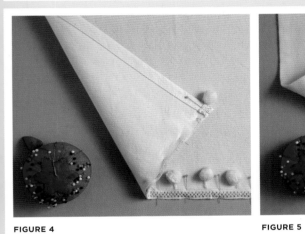

FIGURE 4

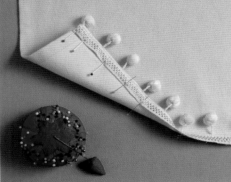

FIGURE 5

FIGURE 6

FIGURE 7

TOO HOT TO HANDLE OVEN MITT

FINISHED SIZE: 11 INCHES BY 7 INCHES

Designed to coordinate with the "Shimmy, Shake & Bake Apron" (page 69), this is one saucy mitt! Essential in every kitchen, you'll want to hang one within easy reach of the stove. Keep your mitt to yourself, or pair it with the apron to make a perfect gift for the pal about to take the plunge—whether that means moving into a new home or enrolling in a cooking class.

WHAT YOU NEED

Enlarge the "Too Hot to Handle Oven Mitt" pattern on page 162 to 400 percent. Convert to a template (see "Preparing the Pattern Pieces" on page 12).

FABRIC

Unbleached cotton canvas: ¼ yard for Mitt Lining

Peacock Blue solid: ¼ yard for Mitt Front and Mitt Back

Blue Geometric print: ⅛ yard for Mitt Front and Mitt Back

OTHER MATERIALS

Tomato Red pom-pom trim: ½ yard
Cotton batting: ¼ yard

SHAPE UP!

Since machine-quilting can sometimes cause distortion of unusual shapes, you'll quilt the front and back of the mitt as rectangles and then cut out the mitt shape.

(CONTINUED)

WHAT YOU DO

1 - Mark the reverse side of the template "Mitt Back." Continue the dotted line from the Mitt Front onto the Mitt Back (Figure 1).

2 - From the batting, cut two 9-inch-by-11¾-inch rectangles. Set aside. From the canvas, cut two 9-inch-by-11¾-inch rectangles for the Mitt Linings. Set aside.

3 - To create the Mitt Fronts and Backs, cut two 9-inch-by-7¾-inch rectangles from the Peacock Blue fabric and two 9-inch-by-4½-inch rectangles from the Blue Geometric print.

4 - Referring to the "String-Piecing Method" on page 16 and with right sides together, stitch one solid rectangle to one print rectangle along the 9-inch-long sides, and press. You will now have a pieced rectangle that measures 9 inches by 11¾ inches. Set aside. Repeat with other solid and print rectangles (Figure 2).

5 - Aligning the template's dotted line with the seam line, lay the Mitt Front template on the right side of one of the pieced rectangles. Trace the template with chalk or a pencil. Set marked rectangle aside. Aligning the dotted line with the seam line, lay the Mitt Back template on the right side of the other pieced rectangle and trace (Figure 3).

6 - Prepare for machine-quilting as follows: Sandwich a layer of batting between the Mitt Front (right side up) and the Lining (wrong side up). (See "Making the Quilt Sandwich" on page 20.) Pin around the perimeter of the rectangle to prevent the layers from shifting as you stitch. Set aside. Layer the Mitt Back rectangle, batting, and lining pieces. Pin around the perimeter.

7 - Machine-quilt the Mitt Front as follows: Set your machine's stitch length to about 10 stitches per inch, and stitch a vertical line down the center of the rectangle from one end to the other. There is no need to backstitch, as you will be cutting through the stitches later. Continue to stitch vertical (but not necessarily parallel) lines on each side of your first vertical line at ½-inch to 1½-inch intervals (Figure 4). Now stitch a horizontal line through the center width of the rectangle. Continue stitching, adding horizontal lines on each side of the first horizontal line at ½-inch to 1½-inch intervals, as you did before. Set the quilted rectangle aside. Repeat Step 7 for the Mitt Back.

8 - Cut out the Mitt Front and Mitt Back along the chalked outlines. With right sides together and the seam lines and edges aligned, pin the Mitt Front to the Mitt Back. Using a ¼-inch-wide seam allowance, stitch from the base of the Mitt up to and around the thumb, over the hand, and down the other side to the base of the Mitt. Clip the curved seam allowances between the thumb and the hand (Figure 5) to smooth out the curved edge. Press open the seam allowances at the Mitt base.

9 - Machine-baste around the raw edge of the Mitt, ⅛ inch from the edge. Turn up the raw edge of the Mitt base ¼ inch toward the Lining side of the Mitt and pin. Topstitch (see page 26) in place to create an unfinished hem. Pin the pom-pom trim along this hem to cover the raw edge, making certain the pom-poms extend just beyond the hem of the Mitt (Figure 6). Cut the end of the trim so the ends overlap 1 inch. Fold under the topmost end ½ inch to prevent it from raveling. Pin in place. To secure the trim, stitch along both edges of the pom-pom trim tape through all layers, backstitching at the beginning and end of the seam to secure the stitches.

10 - Turn the Mitt right side out. To smooth out the curves, roll the seam edges between your fingers. Press flat.

FIGURE 1

FIGURE 2

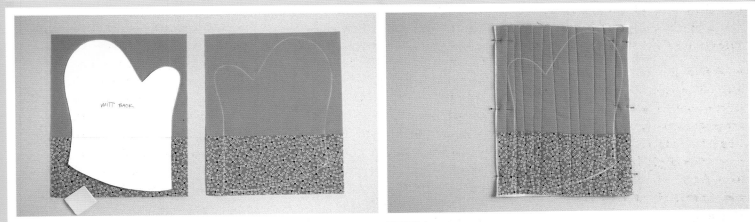

FIGURE 3

FIGURE 4

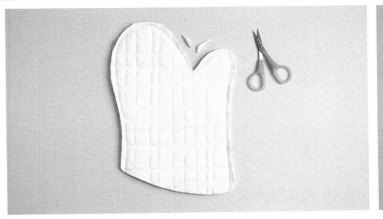

FIGURE 5

FIGURE 6

THREE FACES OF STEVE

FINISHED SIZE: 11½ INCHES BY 5½ INCHES

Steve is one (or two, or even three) cute cat(s)! With one pattern you can create as many different cats as your imagination will allow. Depending on your choice of fabric, buttons, and accessories, he can look wise, rakish, silly, or debonair. You'll be amazed at how simple differences in materials will completely alter his personality. Make Steve from any wool, cotton, or upholstery remnants—or use a slightly stretchy fabric to make a slightly pudgy Steve. If you plan to give Steve to a child, substitute felt circles for the button eyes, for safety.

WHAT YOU NEED

Enlarge the "Three Faces of Steve" pattern on page 159 to 250 percent (see "Preparing the Pattern Pieces" on page 12).

FABRIC

Green wool: ½ yard for the Body
Pink/Green print: about 5 inches by 4 inches for the Ear Accents and Tummy Center
Pink felt: small scrap for the Nose

OTHER MATERIALS

Pink buttons: one small and one large for the Eyes
Pink embroidery floss: one skein for the Mouth and Paws
Pink ribbon: 24 inches for the Bow
Polyfill: 5 ounces for the stuffing

(CONTINUED)

WHAT YOU DO

1 - Referring to "Laying Out and Cutting" on page 13, lay out and pin the enlarged pattern pieces to the right sides of the appropriate fabrics. Cut out all the pieces. Set all the pieces aside, except the Body Back. Using a fabric-marking pencil or dressmakers' chalk, mark the Body Back for placement of the Legs, Tail, and Ears.

2 - From the Green wool, cut two 3-inch-by-12-inch rectangles for the Legs and one 2½-inch-by-11-inch rectangle for the Tail. With right sides together, fold the rectangles in half lengthwise and stitch each piece to create three tubes. Backstitch at the beginning and end of the seams to secure the stitches. Using a safety pin or turning tool, turn the tubes right side out (Figures 1, 2, and 3).

3 - Cut both 12-inch-long tubes in half. You will now have five tubes—four shorter ones for Legs and one long one for the Tail. Stuff each tube with poly filling, and stitch one end of each tube closed, centering the seam. Trim the stitched end with pinking shears. Set the tubes aside (Figure 4).

4 - Using the "String-Piecing Method" (see page 16), stitch the Tummy Left to the Tummy Center, then the Tummy Center to the Tummy Right (Figure 5).

5 - Stitch the Head Front piece to the top edge of the Tummy panel and the Bottom Front piece to the bottom edge of the Tummy panel. Press.

6 - Stay stitch (see page 26) around the perimeter of the Body Front and the Body Back, ⅛ inch from the edge (Figure 6).

7 - To mark the face features, prepare the Head Front pattern by placing it on a semi-soft surface (your ironing board is perfect). Then, with a pushpin, make pinholes along the outline of the nose and mouth, every ⅛ to ¼ inch. Make a pinhole at the center of the eyes to mark placement for the buttons. Then lay the pattern, right side up, on the right side of the Body Front, aligning edges. Use the chalk pouncer to transfer the markings (Figure 7).

8 - With *wrong* sides together, place one Ear Accent on each wool Ear piece. Stitch around the pointed edges. Trim the stitched edges with pinking shears.

9 - Using the chalked markings on the Body Back pieces as a guide, pin the Legs in place, allowing each Leg to extend ¼ inch beyond the Body edge. Make sure the long seams at the back of the Legs are *facing* the right side of the Body Back so they won't be backwards when your cat is

finished. Pin the Ears to the Body Back as marked, with the raw edges aligned with the outer edge of the Head, Ear Accent fabric side up (Figure 8). Machine-baste the Legs and Ears to the Body Back.

10 - With right sides together, lay the Body Front on top of the Body Back, aligning the edges and pinning. Leaving a 2-inch-wide opening on one side for turning, stitch around the perimeter of the Body, backstitching at the beginning and end of the seam to secure the stitches.

11 - Turn the Body right side out through the opening. To smooth the curves, roll the seam edges between your fingers. Press flat to finish. Stuff the Body with poly filling. Close the opening with slip stitches (see page 27).

12 - Using a backstitch (see page 27), embroider the mouth. Attach the nose with tiny whipstitches (see page 27). Sew on the buttons for the eyes. For the toes, whipstitch or blanket stitch (see page 28) the ends of the Legs with embroidery floss (Figure 9). Tie the ribbon around the neck.

13 - To finish the edge of the Tail that will attach to the body, turn in ½ inch of the raw end of the Tail. Using tiny whipstitches, sew the Tail to the back of the cat.

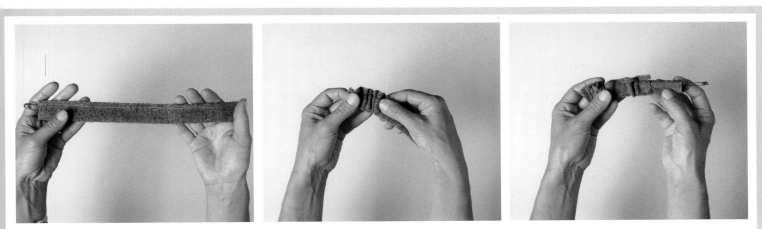

FIGURE 1

FIGURE 2

FIGURE 3

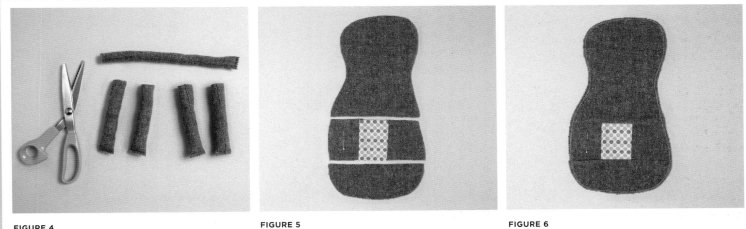

FIGURE 4

FIGURE 5

FIGURE 6

FIGURE 7

FIGURE 8

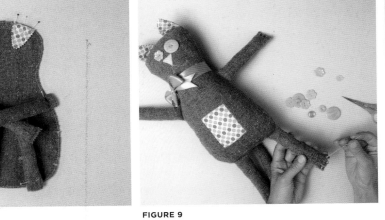

FIGURE 9

SKIRTING THE ISSUE

Being short of cash is no reason to be short on dash. Create a pretty appliqué bouquet to dress up that ho-hum skirt (bag, pillow, or shirt) you picked up at the flea market. Use wool felt, which doesn't fray, eliminating the need for turning under edges. Just cut out the shapes and stitch them on! Felt comes in a wide assortment of colors, so have fun creating blooms in a palette to match your wardrobe. If you have a collection of vintage buttons, consider using stacks of buttons for the flower blooms instead. Dry-clean only.

GET THERE FROM A SQUARE
The easiest way to cut a circle from the felt is to first cut a square the desired size, then "round" the corners.

WHAT YOU NEED
Enlarge the "Skirting the Issue" appliqué pattern on page 160 to 200 percent (see "Preparing the Pattern Pieces" on page 12).

FABRIC
Less than ⅛ yard total of wool felt pieces or scraps, comprising the following (or your preferred) colors:

Medium Green: about 2 inches by 3 inches for the Leaves

Dark Green: about 12 inches by 1 inch for the Stems

Red: about 2 inches by 4 inches for the Outer Blooms

Gold: about 3 inches by 3 inches for the Inner Blooms

Pink: about 2 inches by 2 inches for the Centers

OTHER MATERIALS
Skirt
Lime Green dual-purpose thread
Medium Green dual-purpose thread
Black embroidery floss

(CONTINUED)

WHAT YOU DO

1 - Prepare the pattern for transfer by placing it on a semi-soft surface (your ironing board is perfect). Then, with a pushpin, make pinholes along the center lines of the stem and leaves every $\frac{1}{2}$ inch or so. Make pinholes at the "X" in the center of each bloom. Set aside.

2 - To make the Leaves, cut five 2-inch-by-$\frac{1}{2}$-inch rectangles, then trim the ends to points using the pattern as a guide for the shape.

3 - For the Stems, cut one $\frac{1}{8}$-inch-by-12-inch strip, one $\frac{1}{8}$-inch-by-5$\frac{1}{2}$-inch strip, and one $\frac{1}{8}$-inch-by-3$\frac{3}{4}$-inch strip.

4 - For the Outer Blooms, cut three circles: two that are 1$\frac{3}{8}$ inches in diameter and one that is 1$\frac{1}{4}$ inches in diameter. For the Inner Blooms, cut three circles: two that are $\frac{7}{8}$ inch in diameter and one that is $\frac{1}{2}$ inch in diameter. For the Centers, cut three circles: two that are $\frac{1}{2}$ inch in diameter and one that is $\frac{3}{8}$ inch in diameter.

5 - Position the pattern on the skirt. Use the chalk pouncer to transfer the pattern markings onto the skirt (Figure 1).

6 - Position the long Center Stem on the skirt using the chalk marks as guides, with $\frac{1}{2}$ inch of the Stem extending beyond the hem of the skirt. Turn this part of the Stem toward the inside of the skirt and backstitch the end to secure it to the hem. Using $\frac{1}{4}$-inch-long stitches, hand-baste through the center of the entire length of the Stem.

7 - With the Lime Green thread, couch stitch (see page 28) the entire length of the Stem (Figure 2). Remove the basting thread.

8 - Position the two side Stems on the skirt. Trim the ends at an angle so they are flush with the edge of the Center Stem. Hand-baste through the centers of each of the Side Stems, as you did with the Center Stem (Figure 3). Then couch stitch with Lime Green thread. Remove the basting thread.

9 - Position the leaves on the skirt. Using small whipstitches (see page 27), appliqué the leaves to the skirt with Medium Green thread. Using Lime Green thread, stitch through their centers with a running stitch (see page 26).

10 - To create petals on the blooms, clip tiny notches about $\frac{1}{8}$ inch to $\frac{3}{16}$ inch deep around the circumferences of each of the Outer Blooms and Inner Blooms (Figure 4). (Do not notch the Centers.)

11 - Create the flowers by stacking each Inner Bloom on top of an Outer Bloom of corresponding size, then add a Center. Using three strands of embroidery floss, secure the blooms to the skirt with French knots (see page 27). We used six French knots for the larger blooms and three for the small one.

FIGURE 1

FIGURE 2

FIGURE 3

FIGURE 4

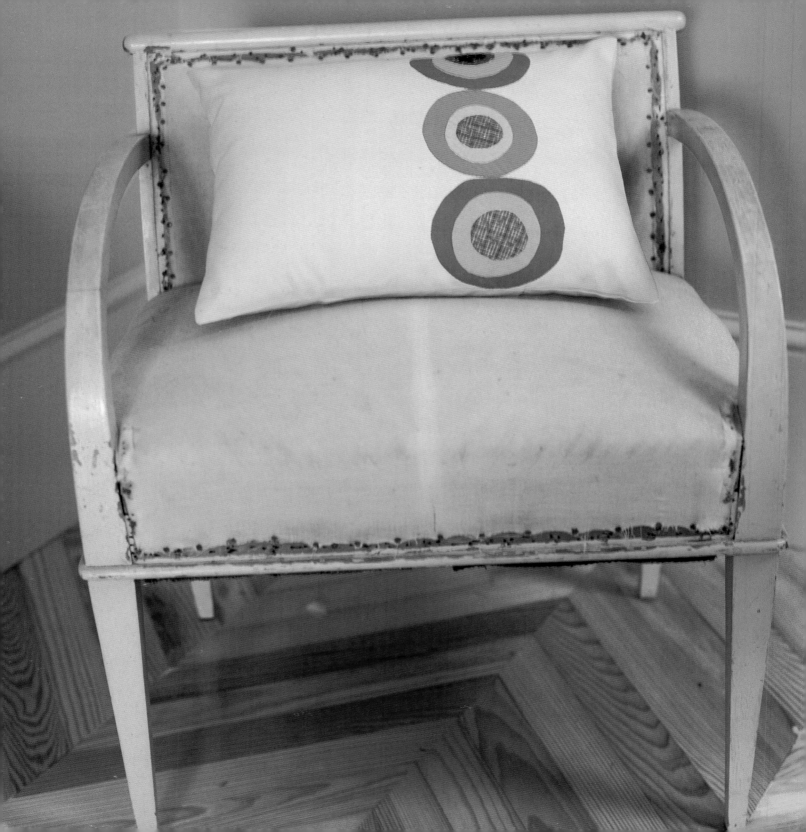

HITS THE SPOT CUSHION

FINISHED SIZE: 12 INCHES BY 16 INCHES

Bullseye! These slightly wobbly, ever-so-off-center appliqué circles make the perfect pillow target for your weary head. This unexpected burst of brightness hits the spot in any room in the house. The cushion cover features an overlapped envelope closure on the back so you can easily remove it for cleaning.

WHAT YOU NEED

Enlarge the "Hits the Spot Cushion" pattern on page 160 as follows (see "Preparing the Pattern Pieces" on page 12):

Center, A, B, and C for Top Bullseye, enlarge to 200 percent.

Center, A, and B for Middle Bullseye, enlarge to 266 percent.

A, B, and C for Bottom Bullseye, enlarge to 214 percent.

Note: There are three bullseyes: Top, Middle, and Bottom. Make sure to mark each pattern piece for Top, Middle, and Bottom after you enlarge them!

FABRIC

Warm Beige cotton canvas: ¾ yard for cushion front and back

A total of about ⅛ yard of cotton fabric pieces, scraps, or remnants, made up of the following (or your preferred) colors:

Poppy Red solid: 5-inch-by-9-inch rectangle for Top Bullseye-C and Middle Bullseye-B

Pumpkin Orange solid: 5-inch-by-5-inch square for Bottom Bullseye-C

Bright Orange solid: 4-inch-by-10-inch rectangle for Top Bullseye-B, Middle Bullseye-A, and Bottom Bullseye-B

Turquoise ikat or plaid: 2½-inch-by-7-inch rectangle for Top Bullseye-A, Middle Bullseye-Center, and Bottom Bullseye-A

Black print: 2-inch-by-2-inch square for Top Bullseye-Center

OTHER MATERIALS

Cushion form: 12 inches by 16 inches

(CONTINUED)

WHAT YOU DO

1 - For the Cushion Front, cut one 12½-inch-by-16½-inch rectangle from the canvas. For the Cushion Backs, cut two 12½-inch-by-12½-inch squares from the canvas. Double-turn a ½-inch-wide hem (see page 26) on one side of each of the Cushion Back squares (Figure 1). Set all Cushion Front and Back pieces aside.

2 - Referring to "Laying Out and Cutting" on page 13, lay out all pattern pieces on the right sides of their respective fabrics, and pin. Cut out all of the Bullseye pieces, and separate them into Top Bullseye, Middle Bullseye, and Bottom Bullseye stacks.

3 - Position each circle for each Bullseye using the dotted lines on the pattern as a guide, and pin through each stack to hold the circles in place.

4 - Referring to "Appliqué" on page 27, mark a light pencil line 3/16 inch from the edge on each circle (Figure 2).

5 - Appliqué the smallest circle in each stack to the one beneath it, and then appliqué each medium circle to the one beneath it, and so on, to create the Bullseyes (Figure 3).

6 - After you've appliquéd all the small and medium circles, you're ready to appliqué the Bullseyes to the Cushion Front. Position the Top Bullseye on the right side of the Cushion Front, 4 inches from the right edge and about ¼ inch from the top edge, and pin. Position the Middle Bullseye below it, with the pencil lines on each large circle just meeting. Pin. Then position the Bottom Bullseye below the Middle Bullseye, about ¼ inch from the bottom edge, with the pencil lines on each large circle just touching (Figure 4). Appliqué each Bullseye to the Cushion Front. Press.

7 - With right sides together, lay one Cushion Back on the Cushion Front, raw edges aligned and the hemmed edge facing toward the center. Pin. With right sides together, lay the second Cushion Back on the Cushion Front, raw edges aligned and the hemmed edge facing toward the center. Pin. (See Figure 5.) Using a ½-inch-wide seam allowance, stitch around the perimeter of the cushion cover.

8 - Turn the cushion cover right side out. Use a point turner to push out the corners (see "Trimming and Point Turning" on page 29). Press flat and then insert the pillow form.

FIGURE 1

FIGURE 2

FIGURE 3

FIGURE 4

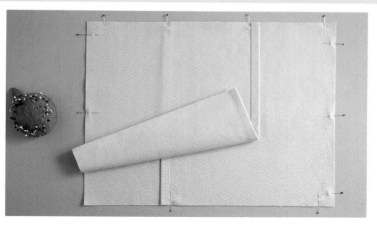

FIGURE 5

STEP LIVELY SLIPPERS

Take your first and last steps of the day in these vibrant, easier-to-make-than-you-think slippers. Your morning trip to the shower becomes just a little brighter, and your nightly, last obsessive check of the stove and locks more fashionable.

IF THE SHOE DOESN'T FIT

The instructions here are for three different women's sizes: S (5–6), M (7–8), L (9–10). The yardages provided here are for the largest size. So, if you want to make a size small, you will have scraps left over.

WHAT YOU NEED

Enlarge the "Step Lively Slippers" pattern on page 162 as follows (see "Preparing the Pattern Pieces" on page 12):

For size small (size 5–6), enlarge all Sole and Upper pattern pieces to 365 percent.

For size medium (size 7–8), enlarge all Sole and Upper pattern pieces to 385 percent.

For size large (size 9–10), enlarge all Sole and Upper pattern pieces to 405 percent.

Note: Make two copies of the Sole pattern piece, as you'll use one for the Lining pieces and one for the Sole pieces (see Step 2, page 90).

FABRIC AND OTHER MATERIALS

Red-Eye solid: about ¼ yard for the Upper Linings

Muslin: about ¼ yard for the Upper Backings

Cotton batting: ¼ yard for the Upper stuffing

High-loft polyester batting: ½ yard for the Sole stuffing

Perky Pink vinyl: ¼ yard for the Soles

Funky Green print: ¼ yard for the Sole Linings

FOR THE UPPERS

A total of about ⅓ yard of cotton fabric pieces, scraps, or remnants, comprising the following (or your preferred) colors:

Eye-Popping Pink print: about 7 inches by 10½ inches for the Upper A pieces

Electric Yellow plaid: about 4 inches by 10½ inches for the Upper B pieces

Perky Pink solid: about 6 inches by 10½ inches for the Upper C pieces

(CONTINUED)

WHAT YOU DO

1 - Referring to "Laying Out and Cutting" on page 13, lay out and pin the Slipper Upper Lining pattern on the Red-Eye fabric, and cut out two pieces for the Upper Linings. From the muslin, cut two 6-inch-by-11-inch rectangles for the Upper Backings. From the cotton batting, cut two 6-inch-by-11-inch rectangles for the Uppers. Set aside.

2 - Cut out one copy of the Sole pattern along the solid, outermost line. Use this pattern for the Sole Lining pieces. Cut out the other copy along the dashed inner line. Use this pattern for all the Sole pieces.

3 - Referring to "Laying Out and Cutting," lay out and pin the Sole pattern on the batting. Cut four Sole pieces from the polyester batting. Set aside.

4 - Use the Sole pattern to cut two Sole pieces from the vinyl. Don't pin the pattern piece to the vinyl for this step, however, as this will leave permanent pin marks. Instead, use a pencil or dressmakers' chalk to trace the Sole pattern, right side up, onto the wrong side of the vinyl. Flip the pattern over (to create the left foot) and trace again. Cut out both Soles and set aside.

5 - Fold the Funky Green print in half, with right sides together. Referring to "Laying Out and Cutting," lay out the Sole Lining pattern on the folded fabric, pin, and cut out to make two Sole Linings (one each for the right and left).

6 - Center the Sole pattern piece on top of the wrong side of one Funky Green Sole Lining. Use a fabric-marking pencil or dressmakers' chalk to trace around the pattern piece. Flip the pattern over and repeat with the other Sole Lining. Stay stitch (see page 26) along the marked line on each Sole Lining.

7 - Machine-baste about $1/8$ inch from the raw edge of the heel and toe of each Sole Lining, leaving long thread ends. Create a second row of machine-basting, this time a generous $1/4$ inch from the raw edge. You will now have two rows of machine-basting (Figure 1). Gather the heel and toe stitching slightly by pulling on the thread ends until the raw edges turn under (toward the wrong side) of each Sole Lining (Figure 2). Use your fingers to arrange the turned fabric until it is flat and evenly distributed around the curves. Tuck two layers of polyester batting into the turned edges of each Sole Lining, using the stay stitching as a guide for placement. Whipstitch (see page 27) the raw edges of the Sole Linings to the batting (Figure 3).

8 - Fold each of the three rectangles of fabrics you will be using for the Upper A, Upper B, and Upper C pieces in half lengthwise, with the right sides together. This allows you to cut the right Upper and left Upper pieces simultaneously. Referring to "Laying Out and Cutting," lay out and pin the Upper A, B, and C pieces to the fabrics. Cut out the pieces, and then arrange them in "Ready-Set-Sew" positions (see page 14) for the left

Upper and the right Upper. To prevent confusing the pieces that belong to each foot, mark all the right-reading pieces with a pin. These will be the pieces you'll need for the right foot. (See figure 4.)

9 - With right sides together, stitch the pieces for the right and left Uppers using the "String-Piecing Method" on page 16. Press the seams toward the Pink fabrics.

10 - Prepare the Uppers for machine-quilting by sandwiching a layer of cotton batting between each pieced Upper (right side up) and a muslin rectangle. Pin the outer edges, and machine-quilt a grid as follows: Set your stitch length to about 10 stitches per inch and stitch a vertical line down the center of the rectangle from one end to the other. There is no need to backstitch, as you will cut through the stitches later. Continue to stitch vertical (but not necessarily parallel) lines on either side of your first line at $1/4$-inch to $3/4$-inch intervals (Figure 5). Next, stitch a horizontal line through the center width of the rectangle, and then continue stitching horizontal lines on either side of the first line at $1/2$-inch to $1\,1/2$-inch intervals, as above (Figure 6). Set aside. Repeat with the second Upper.

11 - Lay the Slipper Lining pattern piece on top of the quilted right Upper. Trace around the edges and cut out the right Upper. Repeat for the left Upper (Figure 7).

FIGURE 1 **FIGURE 2** **FIGURE 3** **FIGURE 4**

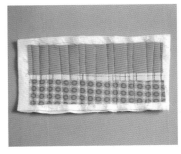 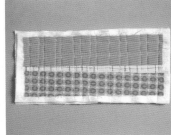  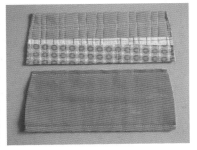

FIGURE 5 **FIGURE 6** **FIGURE 7** **FIGURE 8**

FIGURE 9 **FIGURE 10** **FIGURE 11**

12 - With right sides together, pin one Red-Eye Upper Lining to each of the quilted Uppers. Using a ¼-inch-wide seam allowance, stitch along the two longer sides. Turn right side out, and press. Machine-baste the open ends of each Upper after turning (Figure 8).

13 - Using the dotted lines printed on the Sole Lining pattern piece as a guide, position and then pin each Upper to its respective Sole Lining. (Both the Uppers and the Sole Linings should be right sides up; Figure 9.) With the wrong side of the Slipper facing you, whipstitch the raw edges of the Upper to the Sole batting (Figure 10).

14 - With wrong sides together, pin the edges of the Sole to the Sole Lining. Make sure you pin parallel and close to the outer edge, so that the stitching will hide the pin marks on the vinyl. Edgestitch (see page 26) around the perimeter through all layers, being careful to catch only the outer edges of the Uppers (Figure 11). Add a second row of stitching just inside the first.

HOLD ME CLOSE HEATING PAD COVER

FINISHED SIZE: 12½ INCHES BY 15½ INCHES

Sometimes the stress of everyday living can leave your mind weary and your muscles sore. The bright and cheery Hold Me Close Heating Pad Cover will warm your heart while soothing the pain. You may grow as fond of it as a lover or a pet (if not more), but don't get too cozy and fall asleep with it on!

WHAT YOU NEED

Enlarge the "Hold Me Close Heating Pad Cover" pattern on page 161 to 400 percent (see "Preparing the Pattern Pieces" on page 12).

FABRIC
FOR THE FRONT

A total of about ½ yard of cotton fabric pieces, scraps, or remnants, comprising the following (or your preferred) colors:

Red Hot Reds: about 8 inches by 13 inches total, comprising three different shades of red fabrics for Center and C pieces (we used a medium-scale print, a red solid, and a red yarn-dyed plaid)

Feel Good Greens: about 5 inches by 11 inches total, comprising two different green fabrics for A pieces (we used an aqua solid and a green grass solid)

Cheery Yellows: 9 inches by 11 inches total, comprising four different yellow fabrics for B pieces (we used one large-scale print, one calico print, one yarn-dyed stripe, and one solid)

Peachy Keen Peaches: about 13 inches by 18 inches total, comprising three different peach fabrics for D pieces (we used one large-scale print and two solids)

FOR THE BACK
Perky print: ½ yard

OTHER MATERIALS
Muslin: ½ yard for the Lining

Cotton batting: ½ yard

Velcro: 6 inches of ½-inch-wide Velcro tape to match the Lining

(CONTINUED)

WHAT YOU DO

1 - From the muslin, cut two 15-inch-by-18-inch rectangles for the Linings. From the batting, cut two 15-inch-by-18-inch rectangles. From the Perky print, cut one 13½-inch-by-16½-inch rectangle for the Back. Set aside.

2 - Referring to "Laying Out and Cutting" on page 13, lay out the enlarged pattern pieces on the right sides of the fabrics and pin in place. Cut out all of the pieces. Arrange them in the "Ready-Set-Sew" position (see page 14).

3 - Referring to the "Modified–Log Cabin Method" on page 15, with right sides together, stitch the Front pieces together. Don't forget to use the "Compass Pin" (see page 15)!

4 - To prepare the Back for quilting, mark a 3-inch grid with your fabric-marking pencil or chalk and an acrylic ruler.

5 - Using the methods described in "Making the Quilt Sandwich" on page 20, sandwich one layer of batting between the Front (right side up) and the muslin Lining. Referring to "Hand-Basting" on page 20, baste the layers together. Sandwich the second layer of batting between the Back and the other muslin Lining. Baste the layers together.

6 - Referring to the "Hand-Quilting Stitch" on page 21, quilt the Front in-the-ditch (see page 20) to accentuate the concentric square design (rather than quilting every seam). Quilt a few additional lines in some of the larger pieces to fill in those areas. Quilt the Back in the grid as marked.

7 - After you have finished quilting, square up (see page 29) both the Front and Back to measure 13½ inches by 16½ inches (Figure 2). Trim ¾ inch of batting from the upper edges of the Front and Back (Figure 3). This will make it easier to turn a hem. Stitching through all layers, machine-baste ¼ inch from the top edges of the Front and Back pieces.

8 - With right sides together, stitch the Front to the Back along the two sides and bottom, using a ½-inch-wide seam allowance. Trim the corners (see page 29), and trim the seam allowances of the side seams at the top to make it easier to turn the hem (Figure 4).

9 - Press seams open. Turn Cover right side out. Double-turn a ½-inch hem (see page 26) toward the inside of the Cover, and pin (Figure 5). Blind stitch (see page 27) in place. Press.

10 - Cut Velcro into three 2-inch-long lengths. Pin the "fuzzy" half of the Velcro pieces as follows: Position one of the three pieces at the center of the cover opening, close to the edge of the hem fold. Position the other two fuzzy pieces ¾ inch inside each side seam. Whipstitch (see page 27) them in place. Repeat this step on the other side of the opening, using the "bristle-like" half of the Velcro pieces (Figure 6). *Note: Instructional photos use contrasting thread color for clarity. Use a matching or complementary thread color when stitching.*

11 - Slip your heating pad into the Cover through the opening, then press the Velcro strips together to keep the pad from coming out.

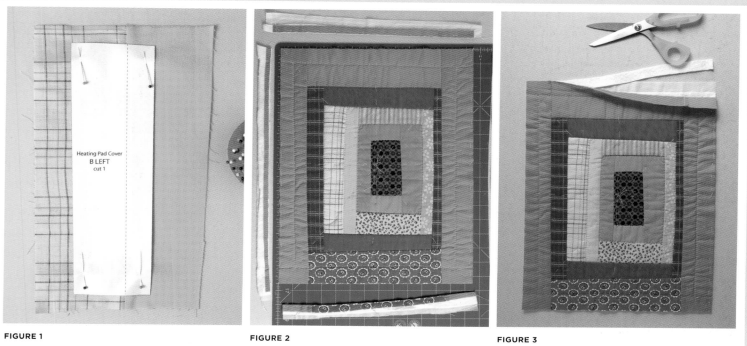

FIGURE 1

FIGURE 2

FIGURE 3

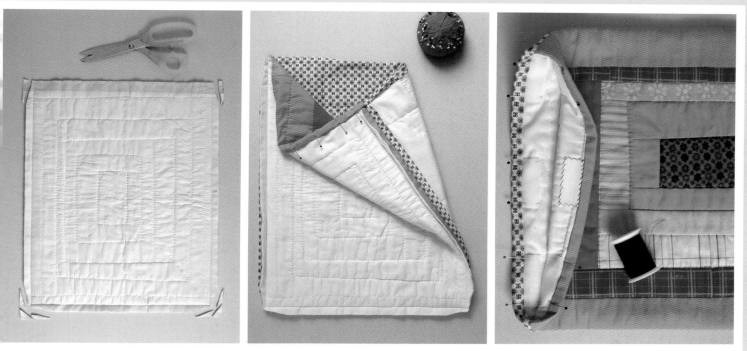

FIGURE 4

FIGURE 5

FIGURE 6

CLOSET CASE SACHET

FINISHED SIZE: 4½ INCHES BY 4½ INCHES

You won't have to hide this moth-repelling aid in the back of the closet. The Closet Case Sachet is as beautiful as it is practical. Slip one of these aromatic sachets over a closet doorknob, clothes hanger, or dresser pull and brighten up the place while the cedar and clove fill keeps the moths from chewing your favorite sweater to bits.

WHAT YOU NEED

Enlarge the "Closet Case Sachet" pattern on page 157 to 200 percent (see "Preparing the Pattern Pieces" on page 12).

FABRIC

FOR THE SACHET BACK AND LINING

Less than ¼ yard of cotton fabric and muslin, comprising the following:

Coral solid: 5 inches by 5 inches for the Back

Muslin or light-color cotton: about 5½ inches by 11 inches for the Lining

FOR THE SACHET FRONT

A total of about ⅛ yard of cotton fabric pieces, scraps, or remnants, comprising the following (or your preferred) colors:

Hot Pink print: about 2 inches by 2 inches for the Center

White solid: about 4½ inches by 3 inches for the A pieces

Blue/Pink stripe: about 6½ inches by 5½ inches for the B pieces

OTHER MATERIALS

Orange seam binding or ribbon: 8 inches
Whole cloves: 1 tablespoon
Cedar chips: ¾ cup

(CONTINUED)

WHAT YOU DO

1 - From the Coral fabric, cut one 5-inch-by-5-inch square for the Sachet Back. From the muslin, cut two 5-inch-by-5-inch squares for the Sachet Lining pieces. Set aside.

2 - Lay out and pin the Front pattern pieces to right sides of the Sachet Front fabrics. Cut out and arrange in the "Ready-Set-Sew" position (see page 14). Remember your "Compass Pin" (see page 15).

3 - Assemble the Sachet Front using the "Modified–Log Cabin Method" (see page 15).

4 - Center one Lining piece on the wrong side of the Sachet Front, and machine-baste around the perimeter just inside the seam allowance. Center the other Lining piece on the wrong side of the Sachet Back, and machine-baste around the perimeter just inside the seam allowance.

5 - Center the seam binding on the right side of the Sachet Front, with the ends extended ½ inch beyond the top edge and 1 inch apart as shown. Pin the binding in place. Machine-baste the ends of the seam binding to the Sachet Front (Figure 1).

6 - With right sides together, lay the Sachet Front on top of the Sachet Back, aligning the edges and pinning, if necessary. Leaving a 1½-inch-wide opening at the center bottom for turning, stitch around the perimeter of the square, pivoting at corners (see "Perfect Corners" on page 28). Backstitch at the beginning and end of the seam to secure the stitches. Trim the corners.

7 - Turn the Sachet right side out through the opening. Use a point turner to push out the corners (see "Trimming and Point Turning" on page 29). Press flat. Fill with the cedar chip and clove mixture (see "Filling It Up" on page 35). Use slip stitches (see page 27) to close the seam opening or stitch by machine close to the edge of the folds.

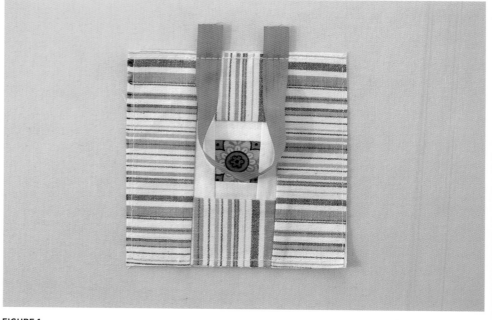

FIGURE 1

BLANKET STATEMENT

FINISHED SIZE: 46 INCHES BY 63 INCHES

This project lets you revive an old blanket (or customize a new one) by hiding its imperfections with bands of color. If you like the way this blanket looks but don't have one in your linen closet, visit a thrift store or Army-Navy surplus store to buy one.

WHAT YOU NEED

FABRIC

A total of about 1¾ yards of cotton fabric pieces, scraps, or remnants, comprising the following (or your preferred) colors:

FOR BAND 1
Orangey Red solid: ¼ yard
Red solid: ¼ yard

FOR BANDS 2 AND 5
Black solid: ¼ yard

FOR BAND 3
Orange solid: ⅛ yard
Orange plaid: ⅛ yard

FOR BAND 4
Orange stripe: less than ⅛ yard
Red solid: less than ⅛ yard (or, leftover fabric from Band 1)

FOR BINDING
Black solid: ½ yard

OTHER MATERIALS
Wool blanket: 46 inches by 63 inches
Orange perle cotton: one ball (45 meters, or 53 yards)

ALL BLANKETS ARE NOT CREATED EQUAL
Your blanket may vary in size from the one shown. The measurements given assume 46 inches by 63 inches. If your blanket is a different size, the instructions explain how to adjust the measurements. If your blanket is wider than 80 inches, you'll need to cut three selvage-to-selvage strips for each band and adjust your fabric yardage accordingly.

(CONTINUED)

WHAT YOU DO

1 - Before you begin, use a rotary cutter to trim off the blanket's original binding (if there is one), and square up your blanket (see "Squaring Up" on page 29).

2 - If your blanket size differs from ours, measure the width of your trimmed blanket. Add 1 inch to this measurement and write it down. Use this measurement for cutting your band lengths.

3 - For Band 1, cut a 5¼-inch-wide strip selvage to selvage from each color (see page 13). With right sides together and placed end to end, stitch the two strips together to make one long strip. Press. Measuring from the Orangey Red end, trim to 47 inches, or the measurement you wrote down in Step 2. You can use the leftover Red fabric for Band 4. Set aside.

4 - For Band 2, cut two 4½-inch-wide strips selvage to selvage from the Black solid. With right sides together and placed end to end, stitch the two strips together to make one long strip. Press. Trim to 47 inches, or the measurement you wrote down in Step 2. Set aside.

5 - For Band 3, cut one 2½-inch-wide strip selvage to selvage from each color. With right sides together and placed end to end, stitch the two strips together to make one long strip. Press. Measuring from the Orange plaid end, trim to 47 inches, or the measurement you wrote down in Step 2. Set aside.

6 - To make Band 4, cut one 1½-inch-wide strip selvage to selvage from each color. Press. Measuring from the Red end, trim to 47 inches, or the measurement you wrote down in Step 2. Set aside.

7 - To make Band 5, cut two 2¼-inch-wide strips selvage to selvage from the Black solid. With Right sides together and placed end to end, stitch the two strips together to make one long strip. Press. Trim to 47 inches, or the measurement you wrote down in Step 2. Set aside.

8 - Turn the long sides of each Band under ¼ inch, and press. Do not turn under the ends (Figure 1).

9 - Arrange the Bands on the blanket, allowing the ends to extend beyond the edge of the blanket and making sure that the seams on the two-color Bands are staggered. Pin them in place.

10 - Referring to the blanket stitch (see page 28), use the perle cotton to stitch the Bands to the blanket. (Our blanket stitches are approximately ¼ inch deep and are spaced about ¼ inch apart.) Secure the knots under the fabric strips, so that they won't show on the back of the blanket. Press the Bands with a dry iron.

11 - Trim the ends of the stripes to align with the edge of the blanket, and machine-baste the raw edges of the Bands through all layers.

12 - Bind the blanket as described in "Binding the Quilt" on page 25.

FIGURE 1

ONE TOTE FITS ALL

FINISHED SIZE: 15 INCHES BY 8½ INCHES BY 13 INCHES

Stash everything you'll need to seize the day—snacks, sneakers, sunscreen, that dog-eared copy of *War and Peace,* and your coordinating "Day at the Beach Quilt" (page 109). You'll need a sewing machine capable of sewing through thick layers for this project, fitted with a heavy-duty needle. If you don't have a machine like this, leave out one layer of the batting.

WHAT YOU NEED

FOR LINING AND INTERLINING

Batting: 2 yards for Interlining

Lightweight canvas: 1 yard for Interlining

Ripe Watermelon cotton solid: 1 yard for Lining

FABRIC
A total of 1⅝ yards of cotton fabric pieces or remnants, comprising the following (or your preferred) colors:

Tar Beach Black solid: ½ yard for Tote Front-A

Lime Cooler solid: 1 yard for Tote Front-B

Almost Black print: ⅛ yard for Tote Front-C

OTHER MATERIALS
Orange Pop lightweight cotton twill tape, 1⅜ inches wide: 5¼ yards for handles and seam binding

(CONTINUED)

WHAT YOU DO

1 - From the batting, cut two 35-inch-by-41-inch rectangles. From the canvas, cut one 35-inch-by-41-inch rectangle for the Interlining. From the Ripe Watermelon, cut one 35-inch-by-41-inch rectangle for the Lining. Set all the pieces aside.

2 - From the Tar Beach Black fabric, cut a 15½-inch-by-30-inch rectangle for the Tote Front-A. From the Lime Cooler fabric, cut two 12½-inch-by-30-inch rectangles for the Tote Front-B. From the Almost Black print fabric, cut two 1-inch-by-30-inch strips for the Tote Front-C.

3 - Referring to the "String-Piecing Method" on page 16, stitch the Tote Front pieces together along the 30-inch-long sides in the following order: B, C, A, C, B.

4 - Referring to "Planning Your Quilting" and "Marking the Quilting Lines" on page 20, prepare your Tote Front for machine-quilting. Using a fabric-marking pencil or dressmakers' chalk, mark an all-over grid pattern, or refer to "Machine-Quilting" on page 23 for information on how to create the figure-eight pattern shown in the photo.

5 - Referring to "Making the Quilt Sandwich" on page 20, layer the pieces in the following order: Front (right side up), batting, canvas Interlining, batting, and Lining (wrong side up) (Figure 1). Referring to "Hand-Basting" on page 20, baste the layers together. Referring to "Machine-Quilting" on page 23, stitch the quilting lines that you marked in Step 4.

6 - After machine-quilting, square up (see page 29) the tote to 36 inches by 25 inches, being sure to center the Front-C strips.

7 - Cut a 3-yard-*plus*-3-inch length of twill tape. Starting with one end at the center, lay the tape out in a long 6-inch-wide oval, creating 19-inch-long loops on each end for the handles. Your 6-inch acrylic ruler makes a great guide for laying out the twill tape. Turn under the remaining end of the tape and overlap it with the first. Pin the whole length of the tape to the Tote (Figure 2).

8 - Stitch each side of the tape on both sides of the oval, stopping 2 inches from the handle ends of the Tote (Figure 3). In Step 15, you'll pick up where this stitching left off.

9 - With right sides together, fold the bag in half, and stitch the sides with a ½-inch-wide seam allowance. Trim 7 inches (starting from the fold) of the side seam allowances to ¼ inch, and trim 1 inch of the seam allowances at the top edges to ¼ inch (Figure 4). Press seams open.

10 - Cut two 10-inch-long pieces of twill tape. They will be used to cover the raw edges of the side seam allowances. Align one end of the twill tape ¾ inch from the top edge of the bag, centering the tape over the raw edges of the side seams, and pin (Figure 5).

11 - Turn the Tote right side out, and using a zipper foot to accommodate the thickness, stitch along both edges of the tape to secure it.

12 - Turn the Tote wrong side out. Flatten the bag at its side seam, centering the seam. With the seam centered, mark a line with dressmakers' chalk across the triangular point, 4 inches from the point (Figure 6). Stitch across the triangular point along the line. Repeat for other side seam.

13 - Fold the point up toward the side seam and blind stitch in place (see page 27) covering the remaining raw edges. Repeat on the other side (Figure 7). Turn the Tote right side out.

14 - To finish the top edge of the Tote, cut a 50-inch length of twill tape for a facing. Fold back one end ½ inch and pin the tape to the Tote's top edge, right sides together, overlapping the tape where the ends meet (Figure 8). Stitch the tape to the Tote with a ½-inch-wide seam allowance. Press the tape toward the seam allowance and stitch close to the seam edge. Fold the tape to the inside of the Tote, and pin (Figure 9). Stitch the free edge of tape through all layers to finish.

15 - Continuing from where the stitching left off in Step 8, stitch both handles to the top edges of Tote. Reinforce by stitching a boxed "X" (Figure 10).

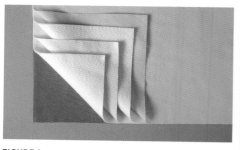

FIGURE 1

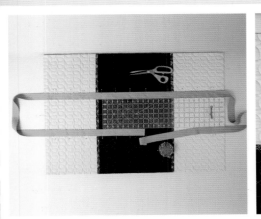

FIGURE 2

FIGURE 3

FIGURE 4

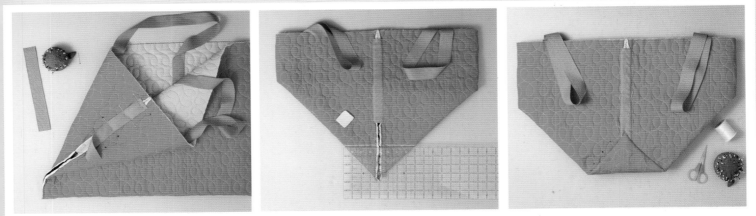

FIGURE 5

FIGURE 6

FIGURE 7

FIGURE 8

FIGURE 9

FIGURE 10

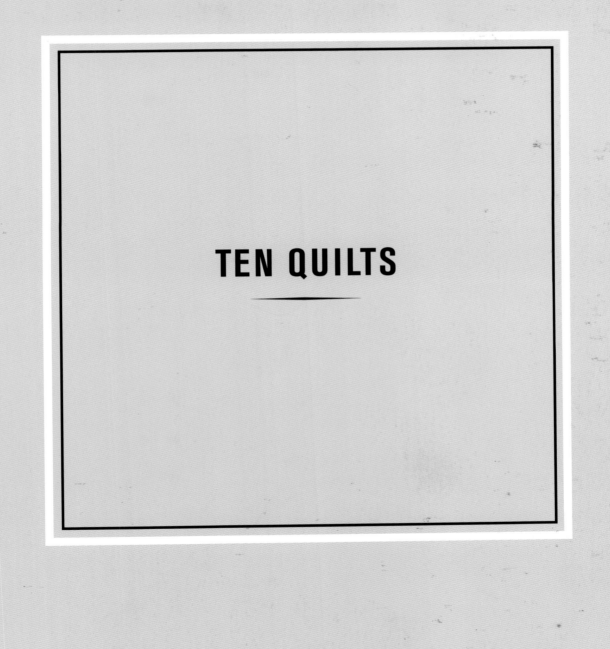

TEN QUILTS

A DAY AT THE BEACH

FINISHED SIZE: 65 INCHES BY 75 INCHES, FOR A THROW-SIZE QUILT
IF YOU'D LIKE TO MAKE THIS QUILT IN A DIFFERENT SIZE, CONSULT THE CHART IN "CHOOSING A QUILT SIZE" ON PAGE 18.

This is an ideal quilt for beginners. Made with large rectangles of color and a single narrow strip, this quilt requires no pattern pieces. The "why-didn't-I-think-of-that" triangular pockets on the back of the quilt hold sand or stones to weight it down and prevent it from flipping over on a windy day. Pair it with the coordinating "One Tote Fits All" (page 103) and make a splash at the shore.

WHAT YOU NEED

FABRIC

FOR THE QUILT TOP

A total of 4⅛ yards of cotton fabric, comprising the following (or your preferred) colors:

Tar Beach Black solid: 2 yards

Sky Blue solid: 2 yards

Almost Black print: less than ⅛ yard for narrow strip

FOR THE QUILT BACK

Lime Popsicle solid: 4 yards, plus ¼ yard for the triangular pockets

FOR THE BINDING

Orange Pop print: ⅓ yard

OTHER MATERIALS

Cotton batting: 70 inches by 80 inches, for a throw-size quilt

GIVE PRE-PIECING A CHANCE

The narrow strip that runs through the center of this quilt can be made with scraps of fabric you have on hand. The instructions here are for a strip comprising two pieces cut from yardage, but you can make the strip out of several fabrics as we have, if you wish. Be sure that your final strip measures at least 65 inches long.

(CONTINUED)

WHAT YOU DO

1 - From the Tar Beach Black, cut a $42\frac{1}{2}$-inch-by-65-inch rectangle for A. From the Sky Blue, cut a $32\frac{1}{2}$-inch-by-65-inch rectangle for C. From the Almost Black print, cut two $1\frac{1}{4}$-inch-wide strips selvage to selvage for B (see page 13).

2 - With right sides together, stitch the two B strips together end to end to make one long strip. Trim to 65 inches. Or try the method in "Give Pre-Piecing a Chance" on page 109.

3 - Using the "String-Piecing Method" on page 16, stitch A to B and B to C (Figure 1). Press. Set aside.

4 - Referring to "Planning Your Quilting" and "Marking the Quilting Lines" on page 20, prepare your Quilt Top for machine-quilting. Using a fabric-marking pencil or dressmakers' chalk, mark an all-over grid pattern or refer to "Machine-Quilting" on page 23 for information on how to create the figure-eight pattern shown in the photo.

5 - Using the methods described in "Constructing a Quilt" that begin on page 18, make a Quilt Back (see page 20), cut the batting (see page 20), then layer the Quilt Back, batting, and Quilt Top (see page 20). Baste the layers together by hand (see page 20) to create the quilt sandwich.

6 - Referring to "Machine-Quilting" on page 23, stitch on the quilting lines that you marked in Step 4.

7 - Square up your quilt (see page 29) to measure 65 inches by 75 inches.

8 - From the Lime Popsicle, cut two 9-inch-by-9-inch squares. Next, cut the squares in half diagonally to make four triangles. These triangles will become pockets for holding weights. Double-turn a $\frac{1}{2}$-inch-wide hem (see page 26) on the long side of each triangle. Position one triangle, right side up, on each corner of the Quilt Back. Pin, then machine-baste each triangle in place $\frac{1}{4}$ inch from the quilt edge, leaving the hemmed side free (Figure 2).

9 - Bind the quilt as described in "Binding the Quilt" on page 25.

10 - Once you've settled on a place in the sand, gather some stones and slip one into each of the triangular pockets. A couple of handfuls of sand serve the same purpose. Even the most persistent gusts won't flip these corners!

A

B

C

FIGURE 1

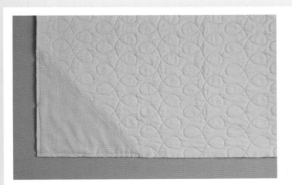

FIGURE 2

FLOCK OF TRIANGLES

FINISHED SIZE: 44 INCHES BY 52 INCHES, FOR A CRIB-SIZE QUILT
IF YOU'D LIKE TO MAKE THIS QUILT IN A DIFFERENT SIZE, CONSULT THE CHART IN "CHOOSING A QUILT SIZE" ON PAGE 18.

As with so many quilt patterns, this one has a thousand faces. The placement of the triangular pieces used here is no different than the ones used for the "Big Zig" quilt (page 141), but alternating colors give this one a completely different appearance. Flock of Triangles is based on the traditional Flying Geese pattern. Some other "trad" designs using triangles include Lightning Stripes and Dutchman's Puzzle. This quilt requires no templates, so you will get lots of rotary-cutting experience.

WHAT YOU NEED

FABRIC
FOR THE QUILT TOP
A total of 2½ yards of cotton fabric, comprising the following (or your preferred) colors:
Marigold Yellow: 1¼ yards (we used five prints and four solids)
Lily White solid: 1¼ yards

FOR THE QUILT BACK
Petunia solid: 2⅛ yards

FOR THE BINDING
Marigold solid: ⅓ yard

OTHER MATERIALS
Cotton batting: 49 inches by 57 inches, for a crib-size quilt

SCRAP HAPPY

If you'd like to use scraps from your fabric stash for this quilt, make triangle-shaped templates for cutting and tracing, rather than using the method described in Steps 1 and 2 on page 114. Referring to "Preparing the Pattern Pieces" on page 12, cut a 6¼-inch square from lightweight cardboard or template plastic. Cut the cardboard square in half from corner to corner. Use one of these triangles for the large triangle template. Cut the second triangle in half, and use one of these triangles for the small triangle template.

(CONTINUED)

WHAT YOU DO

1 - Cut forty-two 6¼-inch Marigold squares. Then, cut the forty-two squares in half diagonally, as shown, to make eighty-four large triangles. Cut fourteen of these triangles in half diagonally to make twenty-eight small triangles (Figure 1). Set all the triangles aside. Be aware that the long side of the triangle will be cut on the bias of the fabric, which can stretch.

2 - Cut forty-two 6¼-inch Lily White squares. Then, cut the forty-two squares in half diagonally to make eighty-four large triangles. Set aside.

3 - Referring to "Arrange the Quilt Blocks" on page 19, arrange the triangles on your design wall or floor in fourteen horizontal rows. Start and end each row with a small Marigold triangle. Fill in the rest with eleven large triangles, alternating six Lily White with five Marigold triangles. If you are using several different Marigold fabrics, arrange the Marigold triangles until you have a good balance of value and patterns (Figure 2).

4 - When you are pleased with your arrangement, refer to "Move 'Em to the Machine" on page 19, and remove the triangles from the wall one row at a time, working from left to right. Stack them and label them Row 1, Row 2, and so on.

5 - Now stitch all the triangles together to make the Rows. Right sides together, align the points where the seam lines intersect on each triangle (Figure 3), and stitch. Avoid pulling or tugging the triangles, as the long sides are bias edges and can stretch. Press all the seams toward the Marigold triangles.

6 - Repeat Step 5 for Rows 2 through 14.

7 - Referring to "Stitch the Rows Together" on page 19, stitch all the rows together. Press.

8 - Referring to "Planning Your Quilting" and "Marking the Quilting Lines" on page 20, prepare your Quilt Top for hand-quilting. We quilted by stitching-in-the-ditch (see page 20) around each white triangle, and stitched eleven vertical quilting lines through the centers of each row of triangles. Use a fabric-marking pencil or dressmakers' chalk to mark the vertical lines. When you stitch-in-the-ditch, there is no need to mark lines.

9 - Using the methods described in "Constructing a Quilt" that begin on page 18, make a Quilt Back (see page 20), cut the batting (see page 20), then layer the Quilt Back, batting, and Quilt Top (see page 20). Baste the layers together by hand (see page 20) to create the quilt sandwich.

10 - Referring to the "Hand-Quilting Stitch" on page 21, stitch on the quilting lines that you marked in Step 8, and stitch-in-the-ditch.

11 - Square up your quilt (see page 29) to measure 44 inches by 52 inches.

12 - Bind the quilt as described in "Binding the Quilt" on page 25.

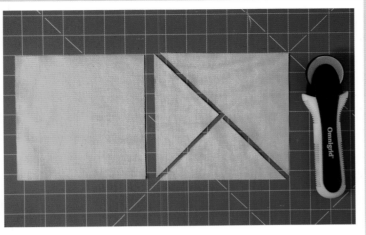

FIGURE 1

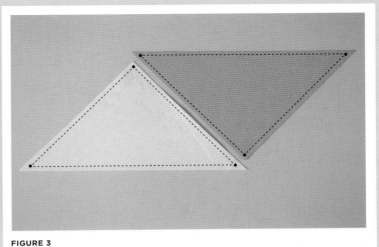

FIGURE 3

FIGURE 2

HOP, SKIP & A JUMP

FINISHED SIZE: 45 INCHES BY 52 INCHES, FOR A CRIB-SIZE QUILT — FINISHED BLOCK SIZE: 13 INCHES BY 14¾ INCHES
IF YOU'D LIKE TO MAKE THIS QUILT IN A DIFFERENT SIZE, CONSULT THE CHART IN "CHOOSING A QUILT SIZE" ON PAGE 18.

Country quilt, meet your city cousin! This quasi-linear design is created in farmhouse colors. Use vintage reds in prints and solids and good, old basic muslin. Your friends will call it downtown chic, but you'll call it down-home comfy.

SEAMS OKAY TO ME

If you want to disguise the block seam lines, cut all your red A and H pieces from the same fabric. Note that each pattern piece in this design except C has at least one slightly curving edge. Use scissors or a 28mm rotary cutter (without the acrylic ruler) to cut the curves. When you put the curved edges right sides together for stitching, they'll appear to not match. Don't panic; it's supposed to be this way! Simply align the raw edges as shown, easing in the fullness (Figures 1, 2, and 3).

WHAT YOU NEED

Enlarge the "Hop, Skip & a Jump" pattern on page 167 to 400 percent (see "Preparing the Pattern Pieces" on page 13).

FABRIC
FOR THE QUILT TOP
A total of 2½ yards of cotton fabric, comprising the following (or your preferred) colors:

Quiltmakers' muslin: 1¼ yards

Note: Quiltmakers' muslin is a superior quality fabric than dressmakers' muslin and is a better choice for your Quilt Top.

Really Red: 1¼ yards (we used seven different prints and two solids)

FOR THE QUILT BACK
Royal Blue solid: 3 yards

FOR THE BINDING
Really Red solid: ⅓ yard

OTHER MATERIALS
Cotton batting: 50 inches by 57 inches, for a crib-sized quilt

(CONTINUED)

WHAT YOU DO

1 - Referring to "Laying Out and Cutting" on page 13 and the colors and quantities listed below, lay out the templates on the right sides of the fabrics. Also see "Seams Okay to Me" on page 117. Trace the templates and cut out the pieces.

For A, C, E, and G pieces: Cut seven each from the muslin.

For B, C, F, and H pieces: Cut five each from the muslin.

For A, C, E, and G pieces: Cut five each from the various Reds.

For B, D, F, and H pieces: Cut seven each from the various Reds.

2 - On a large work surface (a tabletop or the floor), arrange the pieces for the seven blocks with muslin A pieces in the "Ready-Set-Sew" position (see page 14). If you're using several different red fabrics, distribute the Red pieces (keeping each piece in the Ready-Set-Sew position) so that each block has a mix of different solids and/or prints (Figure 4).

3 - To move the block pieces to the machine, slip a piece of paper beneath one of the blocks laid out in the Ready-Set-Sew position (Figure 5), or stack each block's pieces, working left to right, and move the stack to the sewing machine (Figure 6).

4 - Using the "String-Piecing Method" on page 16 and the "Compass Pin" (see page 15), stitch each of the pieces together to create the blocks. Press the seam allowances toward the Red fabrics.

5 - Square up each block (see page 29) to measure 13½ inches by 15¼ inches.

6 - Repeat Steps 2 through 5 for the five blocks with Red A pieces (Figure 7).

7 - Referring to "Arrange the Quilt Blocks" on page 19, arrange the blocks on your design wall or lay them out on the floor. Refer to the photograph of the quilt, or produce a design of your own. If you are using several Red fabrics, as we did, arrange the blocks until you are pleased with the balance of color and pattern. We inverted some of the blocks to make the quilt look less predictable. If you want to disguise the side block seam lines, arrange so that blocks with the same end fabrics are next to each other (Figure 8).

Note: In Figure 8, "BLOCKS" in italics indicates muslin A pieces; "BLOCKS" without italics indicates red A pieces.

8 - When you are pleased with your arrangement, refer to "Move 'Em to the Machine" on page 19, and remove the blocks from the design wall or the floor. Referring to "Blocks into Rows" and "Stitch the Rows Together" (see page 19), stitch the blocks together, and press.

9 - Referring to "Planning Your Quilting" and "Marking the Quilting Lines" on page 20, prepare your Quilt Top for hand- or machine-quilting. Using a fabric-marking pencil or dressmakers' chalk and an acrylic ruler, mark vertical lines every 1¼ inches, or refer to "Machine-Quilting" on page 23 for information on creating the figure-eight pattern shown in the photo.

10 - Using the methods described in "Constructing a Quilt" that begin on page 18, make a Quilt Back (see page 20), cut the batting (see page 20), then layer the Quilt Back, batting, and Quilt Top (see page 20). Baste the layers together by hand (see page 20) to create the quilt sandwich.

11 - To machine-quilt, see page 23. If hand-quilting, use the steps outlined in the "Hand-Quilting Stitch" on page 21, and stitch on the quilting lines that you marked in Step 9.

12 - After you have finished quilting, square up your quilt (see page 29) to measure 45 inches by 52 inches for the crib-size quilt.

13 - Bind the quilt as described in "Binding the Quilt" on page 25.

FIGURE 1

FIGURE 2

FIGURE 3

FIGURE 4

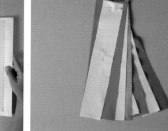
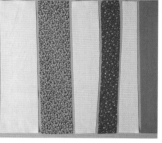

FIGURE 5

FIGURE 6

FIGURE 7

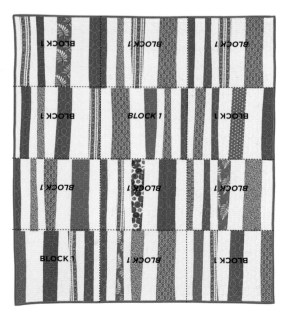

FIGURE 8

ICE POPS

FINISHED SIZE: 80 INCHES BY 88 INCHES, FOR A FULL-SIZE QUILT — FINISHED BLOCK SIZE: 9 INCHES BY 17 INCHES
IF YOU'D LIKE TO MAKE THIS QUILT IN A DIFFERENT SIZE, CONSULT THE CHART IN "CHOOSING A QUILT SIZE" ON PAGE 18.

Set your sights on a tropical paradise just the right size for your bed. Named for frozen sweets and created in colors that suggest mangos, bananas, and coconuts, this quilt is a feast for the eyes. Use various tones of a single hue, like we did here, to give it an inviting glow. Then sink into a little sunshine next time you lie down— even if the moon is overhead.

QUILTING OPTIONS

The quilt in the photograph is hand-quilted in a crosshatch pattern. It looks great with this quilt design, but it is definitely time-consuming. Diagonal quilting will produce equally beautiful results and take only half as long to do. Instructions for both are included here, so choose the pattern that's best for you.

WHAT YOU NEED

Enlarge the "Ice Pops" pattern on page 164 to 400 percent (see "Preparing the Pattern Pieces" on page 13).

FABRIC
FOR THE QUILT TOP
A total of 9¼ yards of cotton fabric, comprising the following (or your preferred colors):
Sand solid: 5½ yards
Coconut solid: 2 yards
Tropical Ice: 1¾ yards, comprising five different fabrics (we used a diagonal print, a yarn-dyed stripe, and three different solids, which are referred to in the instructions as Pineapple, Mango, and Banana)

FOR THE BACK
A total of 5½ yards of cotton fabric, comprising the following (or your preferred) colors:
Coconut solid: 2½ yards
Banana solid: 3 yards

FOR THE BINDING
Banana solid: ¾ yard

OTHER MATERIALS
Cotton batting: 85 inches by 93 inches, for a full-size quilt

(CONTINUED)

WHAT YOU DO

1 - For Top and Bottom Borders: Cut four 10¼-inch-wide strips from Sand solid selvage to selvage (see page 13). Set aside. For Left and Right Borders: Cut five 8¾-inch-wide strips from Sand selvage to selvage. Set aside.

2 - Referring to "Laying Out and Cutting" on page 13 and the colors and quantities listed below, lay out the Quilt Top templates on the right sides of the fabrics. Trace the templates and cut out the pieces. This design works best when all the A pieces within each block are made with the same fabric (Figures 1 and 2). Be sure to cut out all Block 1 pieces first, set aside, then cut out the Block 2 pieces, and set them aside.

FOR BLOCK 1
For the Centers: Cut fourteen from the Coconut.
For the A pieces: Cut fourteen from the Tropical Ices (three each Pineapple, two each Mango, six each Banana, one diagonal print, two each yarn-dyed stripe).
For the B pieces: Cut fourteen from the Coconut.
For the C pieces: Cut fourteen from the Sand.

FOR BLOCK 2
For the Centers: Cut fourteen from the Coconut.
For the A pieces: Cut fourteen from the Tropical Ices (five each Pineapple, two each Mango, three from the Banana, two each diagonal print, two each yarn-dyed stripe).

For the B pieces: Cut fourteen from the Coconut.
For the C pieces: Cut fourteen from the Sand.

3 - Arrange the Block 1 pieces in the "Ready-Set-Sew" position (see page 14). Using a "Compass Pin" (see page 15) and referring to the "Modified–Log Cabin Method" on page 15, stitch all the Block 1 Pops, right sides together. Note that with Ice Pops, the Modified–Log Cabin Method varies somewhat: Long sides are stitched first, and short sides next. Press each block.

4 - Square up each block (see page 29) to measure 9½ inches by 17½ inches. Set them aside.

5 - Repeat Steps 3 through 4 for Block 2 Pops.

6 - Referring to "Arrange the Quilt Blocks" on page 19, arrange the blocks on your design wall, or lay them out on the floor. You can refer to Figure 3 or produce a design of your own. If you are using several fabrics for your Pops, as we did, arrange the blocks so that the colors and textures are distributed throughout the quilt. We alternated Block 1s and Block 2s in each row and inverted the second and fourth rows to make the quilt look less regular.

7 - When you are pleased with your arrangement, refer to "Move 'Em to the Machine" on page 19, and remove the blocks from the design wall or the floor. Referring to "Blocks into Rows" and

"Stitch the Rows Together" (see page 19), stitch the blocks together, and press.

8 - With right sides together and placed end to end, stitch together the four Top and Bottom Border strips to make one long strip. Cut this strip into two 63-inch-long Top and Bottom Borders.

9 - With right sides together and placed end to end, stitch together the five Left and Right Border strips to make one long strip. Cut this strip into two 88-inch-long Left and Right Borders.

10 - With right sides together, stitch the Top and Bottom Borders to the top and bottom edges of the Quilt Top. Press. Next, stitch the Left and Right Borders to the side edges of the quilt. Press.

11 - Referring to "Planning Your Quilting" and "Marking the Quilting Lines" on page 20, prepare the Quilt Top for hand-quilting by making diagonal or crosshatch guidelines. To do so, run a taut length of string from the top left-hand corner to the bottom right-hand corner. Using a fabric-marking pencil or chalk and an acrylic ruler, follow the string and mark parallel diagonal lines with the ruler, at 1¼-inch intervals, until you reach the corners. If want to quilt a diagonal pattern only, proceed to Step 12. If you want to quilt a crosshatch pattern, make another guideline, this time running the string from the top right-hand corner down to the bottom left-hand corner. Following the string, mark parallel diagonal lines at 1¼-inch intervals with the ruler, until you reach the corners.

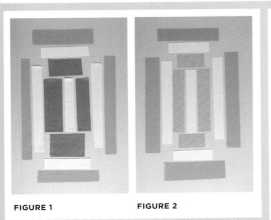

FIGURE 1   **FIGURE 2**

12 - Using the methods described in "Constructing a Quilt" that begin on page 18, make a Quilt Back (see page 20), cut the batting (see page 20), then layer the Quilt Back, batting, and Quilt Top (see page 20). Baste the layers together by hand (see page 20) to create the quilt sandwich.

13 - Referring to the "Hand-Quilting Stitch" on page 21, stitch on the quilting lines that you marked in Step 11.

14 - Square up your quilt (see page 29) to measure 80 inches by 88 inches.

15 - Bind the quilt as described in "Binding the Quilt" on page 25.

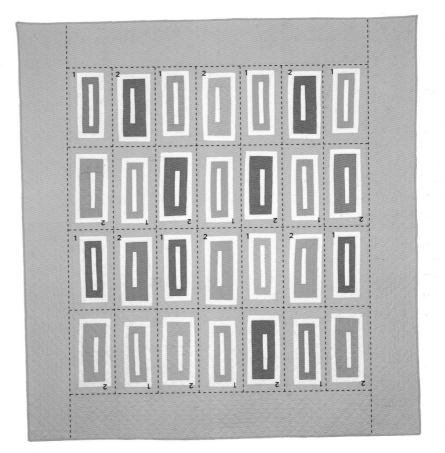

FIGURE 3

ANY WAY YOU SLICE IT

Friends may think you improvised this quilt, making up your design as you drank—uh, worked—but, really, it's made with a pattern. One part psychedelic, one part rustic, and two parts crazy, the fun begins with fifteen colors in a bright and warm palette. We used fabrics in groups of colors—three each of greens, blues, deep browns, red/oranges, and white/yellows. You can use these colors or experiment with a monochrome scheme. For the color-challenged, it's hard to go wrong with this quilt, especially with the angst-free color-mixing method you'll find in the instructions.

CHANGE IN DIRECTION

If you'd like to experiment with variations on this design, try rotating some of the blocks. You can make zigzag rows or an all-over diagonal pattern. Just keep in mind that the Block 1s are a little "wackier" than the Block 2s and 3s, so they should be placed judiciously.

WHAT YOU NEED

Enlarge the "Any Way You Slice It" pattern on page 165 to 400 percent (see "Preparing the Pattern Pieces" on page 13).

FABRIC

FOR THE QUILT TOP

A total of 5 yards of cotton fabric, comprising the following (or your preferred) colors:

Yellow Green: $\frac{1}{3}$ yard each of three different solids

Turquoise Blue: $\frac{1}{3}$ yard each of three different solids

Rich Brown: $\frac{1}{3}$ yard each of two different prints and one solid

Warm Red and Orange: $\frac{1}{3}$ yard each of three different solids

Breezy White and Yellow: $\frac{1}{3}$ yard each of one plaid and two different solids

FOR THE QUILT BACK

Hot Red solid: $3\frac{1}{2}$ yards

FOR THE BINDING

Rich Brown solid: $\frac{1}{2}$ yard

OTHER MATERIALS

High-loft polyester batting: 65 inches by 65 inches, for a throw-size quilt

Cream worsted-weight wool yarn: about 18 yards for the ties

(CONTINUED)

WHAT YOU DO

1 - Prepare the fabrics for Block 3 as follows: Select fourteen of the fabrics, and cut one 12-inch-by-16-inch rectangle from each. With right sides up and the edges aligned, stack the rectangles in two groups of five rectangles and one group of four rectangles. (If you're new to rotary-cutting, stack fewer layers at a time.)

2 - Referring to "Laying Out and Cutting" on page 13, lay out the Block 3 templates on top of one stack of fabrics. Trace, then cut out all of the pieces. Arrange the cut pieces on a large surface, such as a tabletop or the floor, in "Ready-Set-Sew" positions (see page 14). Repeat with the second and third stacks of fabric. You will now have fourteen Block 3s arranged in the Ready-Set-Sew position (Figure 1).

3 - To make each Block 3 color-combination distinctive, shuffle the pieces around until each block has a mix of fabrics and colors. You can work systematically, moving all of the A pieces around first, for instance, then moving the B pieces, and so on. Or, you can improvise, swapping out colors until you're pleased with the results (Figures 2 and 3). Just remember to keep the pieces in the Ready-Set-Sew position as you work. The pieces in the Mix-It-Up Cocktail Coasters are shuffled and arranged in the same manner (refer to Step 4 and Figures 3, 4, and 5 on pages 66–67).

4 - To move the block pieces to the sewing machine, slip a piece of paper (Figure 4) beneath one of the blocks laid out in Ready-Set-Sew, or stack each block's pieces, working left to right, and move the stack to the sewing machine.

5 - Using the "String-Piecing Method" on page 16 and with right sides together, stitch all the Block 3 pieces together, aligning the points where the seam lines intersect on each piece (Figure 5). Press the seam allowances toward the darker colors.

6 - Square up the blocks (see page 29) to measure 10½ inches by 10½ inches. Set aside.

7 - Repeat Steps 1 through 6 using the Block 2 templates. Be sure to substitute the fabric you did *not* include in the Block 3 selection for one of the fabrics in the Block 2 selection.

8 - Block 1 is slightly different than Blocks 2 and 3. There are only eight of these in the quilt shown, and to use all the fabrics, you'll need to divide the templates into two groups for cutting. Prepare the fabrics for Block 1 as follows: From each of fourteen different fabrics, cut *one* 12-inch-by-10-inch rectangle. Then, from the fifteenth fabric, cut *two* 12-inch-by-10-inch rectangles.

You will now have sixteen rectangles of fabric. With right sides up and the edges aligned, stack the rectangles in four groups of four rectangles, making sure each stack has a range of colors.

9 - Lay out only the Block 1-A, 1-C, and 1-E templates on top of one stack of fabrics. Trace, then cut out all of the pieces. Arrange them on a large work surface in the Ready-Set-Sew position, leaving spaces for the 1-B, 1-D, and 1-F pieces. Repeat with a second stack of fabric.

10 - Lay out the Block 1-B, 1-D, and 1-F templates on top of the third stack of fabrics. Trace and cut as you did in Step 2. Next, arrange the cut 1-B, 1-D, and 1-F pieces in the spaces between the 1-A, 1-C, and 1-E pieces you cut out in Step 9. Repeat with the fourth stack of fabric. You will now have eight Block 1s arranged in the Ready-Set-Sew position.

11 - Referring to Steps 3 through 6, move the pieces around to mix up the colors, and then, with right sides together, stitch all the Block 1 pieces together.

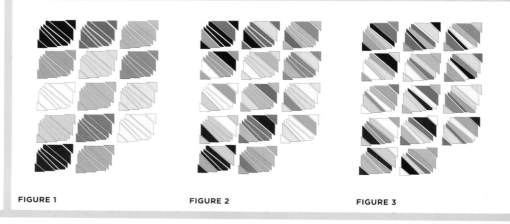

FIGURE 1   FIGURE 2   FIGURE 3

12 - Referring to "Arrange the Quilt Blocks" on page 19, arrange the blocks on your design wall, or lay them out on the floor. You can refer to Figure 6 or produce a design of your own. See also "Change in Direction" on page 125 for ideas.

13 - When you are happy with your arrangement, refer to "Move 'Em to the Machine" (see page 19), and remove the blocks from the design wall or floor. Referring to "Blocks into Rows" and "Stitch the Rows Together" (see page 19), stitch the blocks together, and press.

14 - Referring to "Planning Your Quilting" and "Marking the Quilting Lines" on page 20, prepare your Quilt Top for hand-tying (see page 23). Using a fabric-marking pencil or dressmakers' chalk, mark the center of each block and the center of each block's side seams.

15 - Using the methods described in "Constructing a Quilt" that begin on page 18, make a Quilt Back (see page 20), cut the batting (see page 20), then layer the Quilt Back, batting, and Quilt Top (see page 20). Baste the layers together by hand (see page 20) to create the quilt sandwich.

16 - Referring to "Hand-Tying" on page 23, use the Cream yarn to tie the quilt in the places you marked in Step 14.

17 - Square up your quilt (see page 29) to measure 60 inches by 60 inches.

18 - Bind the quilt as described in "Binding the Quilt" on page 25.

FIGURE 4

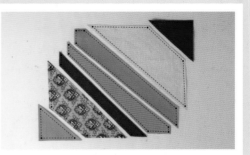

FIGURE 5

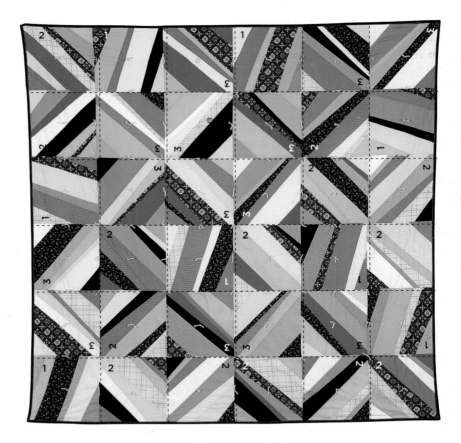

FIGURE 6

WHAT A BUNCH OF SQUARES

FINISHED SIZE: 85 INCHES BY 93 INCHES, FOR A QUEEN-SIZE QUILT — FINISHED BLOCK SIZE: 17 INCHES BY 17 INCHES
IF YOU'D LIKE TO MAKE THIS QUILT IN A DIFFERENT SIZE, CONSULT THE CHART IN "CHOOSING A QUILT SIZE" ON PAGE 18.

The first version of this quilt was created in 1996. The design was completely improvised, no two blocks were the same, and there was no pattern. The version here retains the liveliness of the original, but includes a pattern. To give it more of an "improvised" look, each block pattern is a slightly different size. You'll add a white frame to each block to make them all the same size, wide enough to give you some wiggle room when squaring up the blocks. This way, you can make every block unique (some more off center or slightly askew than others) by trimming them all slightly differently.

WHAT YOU NEED

Enlarge the "What a Bunch of Squares" patterns on page 166 to 400 percent (see "Preparing the Pattern Pieces" on page 13).

FABRIC
FOR THE QUILT TOP
A total of 10 yards of cotton fabric, comprising the following (or your preferred) colors:

Cloud White solid: 6 yards

Lake Blues: ½ yard total, comprising three different blue-toned fabrics (we used three different solids)

Limeade Green solid: 3 yards

Lemonade Yellows: ½ yard total, comprising four different fabrics (we used two yarn-dyed plaids, a print, and a solid)

FOR THE QUILT BACK
Lemonade Yellow solid: 5½ yards

FOR THE BINDING
Lake Blue solid: ¾ yard

OTHER MATERIALS
Cotton batting: 90 inches by 97 inches, for a queen-size quilt

(CONTINUED)

WHAT YOU DO

1 - For the Top and Bottom Borders, cut five Cloud White strips, each 4½ inches wide selvage to selvage (see page 13). Set aside.

2 - Referring to "Laying Out and Cutting" on page 13, lay out the templates on the right sides of the fabrics, trace, and cut out the Quilt Top pieces in the colors and quantities listed below. Be sure to cut out all the Block 1 pieces first, and set them aside. Next, cut out the Block 2 pieces, and set them aside, then cut out the Block 3 pieces.

FOR BLOCK 1
For Centers: Cut eight Lake Blue.

For A-Top pieces: Cut six Limeade Green and two Lemonade Yellow.

For A-Bottom pieces: Cut eight Limeade Green.

For A-Left pieces: Cut six Limeade Green and two Lemonade Yellow.

For A-Right pieces: Cut eight Limeade Green.

For Block 1 Frames: Cut eleven Cloud White strips, each 4½ inches wide selvage to selvage.

FOR BLOCK 2
For Centers: Cut eight Lake Blue.

For A-Top pieces: Cut eight Limeade Green.

For A-Bottom pieces: Cut seven Limeade Green and one Lemonade Yellow.

For A-Left pieces: Cut four Limeade Green and four Lemonade Yellow.

For A-Right pieces: Cut eight Limeade Green.

For Block 2 Frames: Cut eleven Cloud White strips, each 5½ inches wide selvage to selvage.

FOR BLOCK 3
For Centers: Cut nine Lake Blue.

For A-Top pieces: Cut seven Limeade Green and two Lemonade Yellow.

For A-Bottom pieces: Cut eight Limeade Green and one Lemonade Yellow.

For A-Left pieces: Cut nine Limeade Green.

For A-Right pieces: Cut eight Limeade Green and one Lemonade Yellow.

For Block 3 Frames: Cut twelve Cloud White strips, each 5 inches wide selvage to selvage.

3 - Arrange the Block 1 pieces in the "Ready-Set-Sew" position (see page 14). Using a "Compass Pin" (see page 15) and referring to the "Modified–Log Cabin Method" on page 15, stitch all the Block 1 pieces together, and set aside. Position the Block 2 pieces in the Ready-Set-Sew position, stitch, and set aside. Repeat with the Block 3 pieces.

4 - A white "frame" is added to the perimeter of each block using the Modified–Log Cabin Method but no patterns are used. Instead, the white pieces are cut to size as you work. You'll stitch strips to the *seamed* sides of the blocks first. *Note: Blocks 1, 2, and 3 differ slightly in size, so you must use the white strips that are the appropriate width for each block.* Place one block on your cutting mat. From an appropriate white strip, cut two pieces the same length (or a little longer) than the seamed sides of the block (Figure 1). Right sides together, stitch these white pieces to the block's sides, and press. Even up the sides by trimming off any extra fabric from the white pieces (Figure 2).

MAKE LEMONADE
When you're laying out the A pieces in Ready-Set-Sew, don't worry too much about which color goes where. We just stacked the pieces as we cut them and sewed each block together as is. As long as your Lemonade colors are similar in value and hue, they'll work together.

5 - Then, from the white strip, cut two pieces the same length as (or a little longer than) the two remaining sides of the block (Figure 3). Stitch the white pieces to the block's sides, and press. Square up the block (see page 29) to measure 17 ½ inches by 17½ inches (Figure 4). Repeat the step for the remaining blocks. Square up the blocks to measure 17½ inches by 17½ inches. Remember to trim each block a little differently when squaring up (Figure 5). Set aside.

6 - Referring to "Arrange the Quilt Blocks" on page 19, arrange the blocks on your design wall, or lay them out on the floor. You can refer to the diagram on page 133 (Figure 6) or produce a design of your own. Arrange the blocks until you are pleased with the balance of color and pattern. Rotate a few of the blocks to make the design look less regular, and avoid clustering identical blocks in any one area.

7 - When you are pleased with your arrangement, refer to "Move 'Em to the Machine" on page 19, and remove the blocks from the design wall or floor. Referring to "Blocks into Rows" and "Stitch the Rows Together" (see page 19), stitch the blocks together, and press.

(CONTINUED)

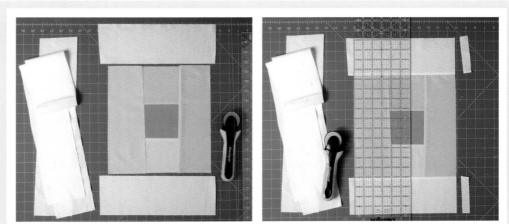

FIGURE 1

FIGURE 2

FIGURE 3

FIGURE 4

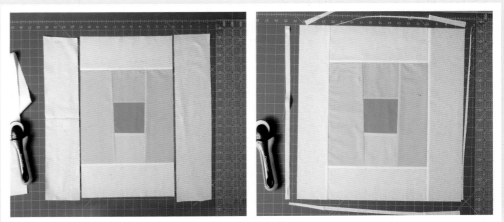

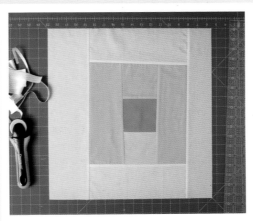

FIGURE 5

8 - With right sides together and placed end to end, stitch together the Top and Bottom Border strips to make one long strip. Cut this long strip into two 85-inch-long Top and Bottom Borders.

9 - With right sides together, stitch the Top and Bottom Borders to the top and bottom edges of the Quilt Top. Press.

10 - Referring to "Planning Your Quilting" and "Marking the Quilting Lines" on page 20, prepare the Quilt Top for hand-quilting as follows: Beginning at the outermost block seams and working toward the center of the block, use a fabric-marking pencil and your acrylic ruler to mark concentric squares every $1\frac{1}{4}$ inches. You will stitch-in-the-ditch around the blue and green squares, so if a marked line falls very close (within $\frac{1}{2}$ inch) of a seam line, there is no need to mark it. For example, in Block 2, you will stitch-in-the-ditch around the center blue squares, rather than where the marked line would have fallen. You will quilt six quilted concentric squares for each block.

11 - On the Top and Bottom Borders, mark a straight line $1\frac{1}{4}$ inches from the seam line and another line $1\frac{1}{4}$ inches from the first on the side that is closer to the raw edge.

12 - Using the methods described in "Constructing a Quilt" that begin on page 18, make a Quilt Back (see page 20), cut the batting (see page 20), then layer the Quilt Back, batting, and Quilt Top (see page 20). Baste the layers together by hand (see page 20) to create the quilt sandwich.

13 - Referring to the "Hand-Quilting Stitch" on page 21, stitch by hand on the quilting lines that you marked in Step 10. Referring to "Stitch-in-the-Ditch Quilting" on page 20, stitch around the block seams and the blue and green squares.

14 - After you have finished quilting, square up your quilt (see page 29) to measure 85 inches by 93 inches.

15 - Bind the quilt as described in "Binding the Quilt" on page 25.

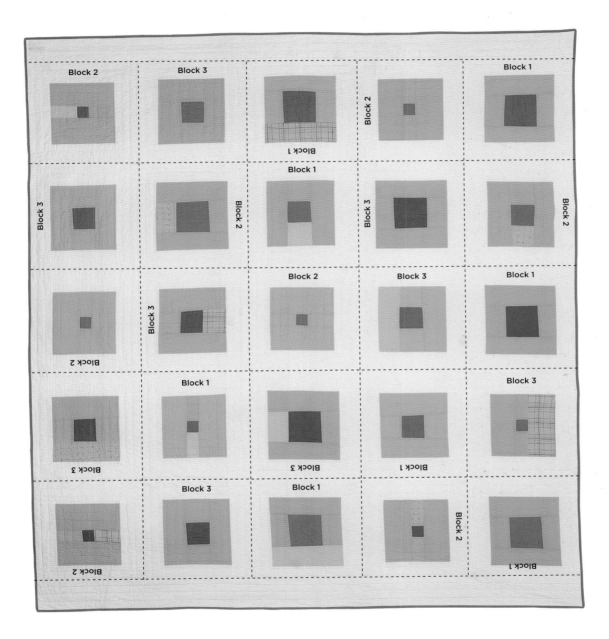

FIGURE 6

SNAKE CHARMER

FINISHED SIZE: 80 INCHES BY 88 INCHES, FOR A FULL-SIZE QUILT — FINISHED BLOCK SIZE: 9¼ INCHES BY 9¼ INCHES
IF YOU'D LIKE TO MAKE THIS QUILT IN A DIFFERENT SIZE, CONSULT THE CHART IN "CHOOSING A QUILT SIZE" ON PAGE 18.

This quilt pattern is a second cousin (twice removed) to a traditional quilting pattern called Snake in the Grass (also Snake in the Hollow, or Drunkard's Trail, depending on the block arrangement). What makes this version distinctive is that it comprises two block designs, whereas the original has only one. If you are new to stitching curves, it's a good idea to cut and sew some practice pieces before you begin. Curves can be tricky at first!

WHAT YOU NEED

Enlarge the "Snake Charmer" pattern on page 167 to 400 percent. Make two enlarged copies of both 2A and 2B pattern pieces. Before converting the pattern to templates, refer to Step 1 of "What You Do" on page 136.

FABRIC
FOR THE QUILT TOP
A total of 7⅞ yards of cotton fabric, comprising the following (or your preferred) colors:

New Grass Green solid: 4⅞ yards

Funky Black: 3 yards total, comprising four different black prints (we used a floral print, a dot print, and two geometric prints)

FOR THE QUILT BACK
Coal Black solid: 5½ yards

FOR THE BINDING
Funky Black print: ¾ yard

OTHER MATERIALS
High-loft polyester batting: 85 inches by 93 inches, for a full-size quilt

Lime Green medium-weight crochet cotton: about 115 yards for the ties

CHECK OUT THESE VALUES!
To ensure that the snake shapes appear as cohesive units in the finished quilt, choose fabrics that are similar in color and value. A ruby glass can help in determining the relative value of your fabric choices. The best way to see what fabrics will work is to lay swatches (or pieces cut with the templates) on a piece of the background fabric, then step back to get an overall view. You'll be surprised at how often something you think will work won't, and vice versa.

(CONTINUED)

WHAT YOU DO

1 - Referring to "Preparing the Pattern Pieces" on page 13, convert *one* set of the Block 2A and 2B pattern pieces into templates. From the other set of the Block 2A and 2B pattern pieces, make mirror-image templates of both by cutting out the paper patterns and transferring the notch marks onto the *reverse side* of the pattern before making them into templates. Glue these pattern pieces to the cardboard or template plastic with the reverse side up. Label these templates "2A-Mirror" and "2B-Mirror" (Figure 1).

2 - Clip out the notches on all the templates so you can mark the notches onto the fabrics.

3 - Referring to "Laying Out and Cutting" on page 13 and the colors and quantities listed below, lay out the Quilt Top templates on the right sides of the fabrics. Trace the templates and cut out the pieces as follows. Then, with a fabric-marking pencil or dressmakers' chalk, mark the pattern notches on all the fabric pieces (Figure 2).

FOR BLOCK 1

For 1A: Cut twelve from the New Grass Green solid.

For 1B: Cut twelve from the Funky Black prints.

For 1C: Cut twelve from the New Grass Green solid.

FOR BLOCK 2

For 2A: Cut thirty-six from the New Grass Green solid.

For 2A-Mirror: Cut thirty-six from the New Grass solid.

For 2B: Cut eighteen from the Funky Black prints.

For 2B-Mirror: Cut eighteen from the Funky Black prints.

4 - For Top Border: Cut two strips from New Grass Green, 3½ inches wide selvage to selvage (see page 13). Set aside. For Bottom Border: Cut two strips from New Grass Green, 12¼ inches wide selvage to selvage. Set aside. For Left and Right Borders: Cut five strips from New Grass Green, 10¼ inches wide selvage to selvage. Set aside.

5 - Arrange the Block 1 pieces in the "Ready-Set-Sew" position (see page 14). The curved pieces will look as though they won't fit together (Figure 3), but this is because there is extra fabric for seam allowances. With right sides together, pin the concave edge of 1A to the convex edge of 1B, matching the notches and easing the fullness of the fabric into the curve. Use as many pins as you need to keep the fabric smooth and the edges aligned (Figure 4). Keeping a flat, consistent ¼-inch-wide seam allowance, stitch 1A to 1B. Press seam allowance toward the B pieces.

6 - Next, with right sides together, pin the concave edge of 1B to the convex edge of 1C, matching the notches and easing the fabric into the curve. Again, use as many pins as you need to keep the fabric smooth and the edges aligned (Figure 5). Keeping a flat, consistent ¼-inch-wide seam allowance, stitch 1B to 1C (Figure 6). Press seam allowance toward the B piece.

7 - Arrange the Block 2 pieces in the Ready-Set-Sew position (Figure 7). Be sure to position half of the 2A pieces to the left of the snake and the rest, rotated 180 degrees, to the right side of the snake. With right sides together, pin 2A to 2B, matching the notches and easing the fabric into the curves. Stitch the pieces together as you did in Step 5 (Figure 8). Press seam allowance toward the B piece.

8 - Next, with right sides together, pin 2B to another 2A piece (this one rotated), matching the notches and easing the fabric into the curves (Figure 9). Stitch the pieces together as you did in Step 5. Press all seam allowances toward the B piece (Figure 10).

(CONTINUED)

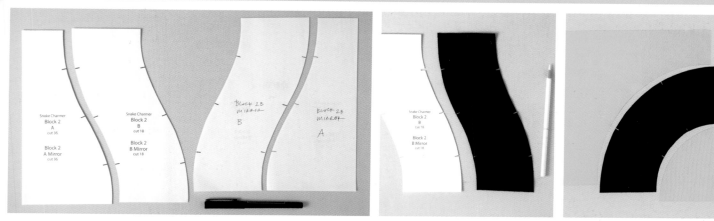

FIGURE 1

FIGURE 2

FIGURE 3

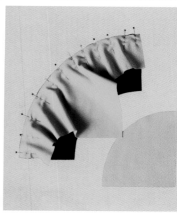

FIGURE 4

FIGURE 5

FIGURE 6

FIGURE 7

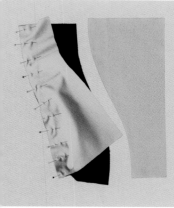

FIGURE 8

FIGURE 9

FIGURE 10

9 - Arrange the Block 2-Mirror pieces in the Ready-Set-Sew position, with half of the 2A-Mirror pieces to the left side of the snake and the rest, rotated 180 degrees, to the right. With right sides together, pin 2A-Mirror to 2B-Mirror, matching the notches and easing the fabric into the curves. Stitch the pieces together as you did in Step 5. Next, with right sides together, pin the 2B-Mirror piece to another 2A piece (this one rotated), matching the notches and easing the fabric into the curves. Stitch the pieces together as you did in Step 5. Press all seam allowances toward the B-Mirror piece.

10 - Square up the blocks (see page 29) to measure 9¾ inches by 9¾ inches.

11 - Referring to "Arrange the Quilt Blocks" on page 19, arrange the blocks on your design wall, or lay them out on the floor. Note that the top and bottom rows of blocks are composed of a horizontal row of six Block 1s. Rotate the blocks as shown in Figure 11 to create the hairpin turns at the ends of the snakes. The rest of the quilt is composed of six horizontal rows of six Block 2s, which must be arranged with standard (non-mirror) Block 2s alternated with mirrored versions of the same. If you are using several different print fabrics for the snake, arrange the blocks to create an interesting interplay of textures.

12 - When you are pleased with your arrangement, refer to "Move 'Em to the Machine" on page 19, and remove the blocks from the design wall or the floor. Referring to "Blocks into Rows" and "Stitch the Rows Together" (see page 19), stitch the blocks together, and press.

13 - With right sides together and placed end to end, stitch together the Top Border strips to make one long strip. Trim the strip to measure 56 inches. Set aside. With right sides together and placed end to end, stitch together the Bottom Border strips to make one long strip. Trim to measure 56 inches. Set aside. With right sides together and placed end to end, stitch together the four Left and Right Border strips to make one long strip. Cut into two 87-inch-long borders. Set aside.

14 - With right sides together, stitch the Top Border and Bottom Border to the top and bottom of the Quilt Top. Press. With right sides together, stitch the Left and Right Borders to the sides of the Quilt Top. Press.

15 - Referring to "Planning Your Quilting" and "Marking the Quilting Lines" on page 20, prepare the Quilt Top for hand-tying as follows: Beginning at the center of the Quilt Top and using the block seams and the markings on your acrylic ruler as guides, mark a 3-inch grid with a fabric-marking pencil or dressmakers' chalk. Make dots at the grid intersections, extending the grid into the border.

16 - Using the methods described in "Constructing a Quilt" that begin on page 18, make a Quilt Back (see page 20), cut the batting (see page 20), then layer the Quilt Back, batting, and Quilt Top (see page 20). Baste the layers together by hand (see page 20) to create the quilt sandwich.

17 - Referring to "Hand-Tying" on page 23, use the Lime Green crochet cotton to tie the quilt as marked in Step 15.

18 - Square up your quilt (see page 29) to measure 80 inches by 88 inches.

19 - Bind the quilt as described in "Binding the Quilt" on page 25.

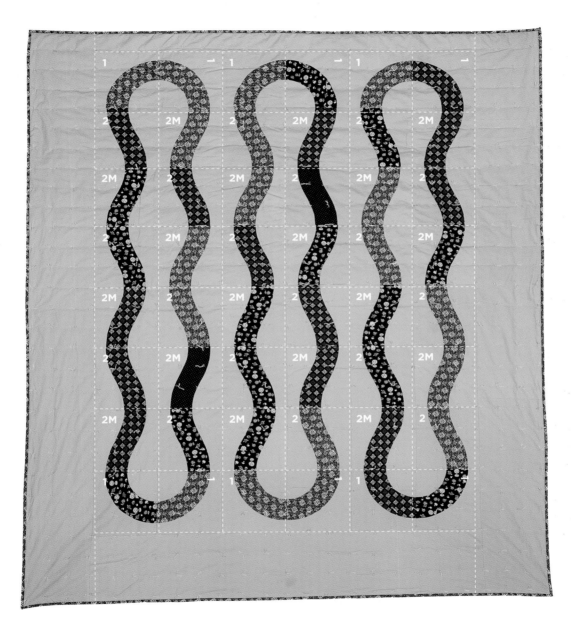

FIGURE 11

BIG ZIG

FINISHED SIZE: 87½ INCHES BY 93 INCHES, FOR A QUEEN-SIZE QUILT

IF YOU'D LIKE TO MAKE THIS QUILT IN A DIFFERENT SIZE, CONSULT THE CHART IN "CHOOSING A QUILT SIZE" ON PAGE 18.

This quilt is so simple, so graphic, and so reminiscent of your favorite childhood shirt. Best of all, it's so darn easy to make. Think of the design as four narrow rows of pieced triangles that result in two zigzags, with a wide strip of fabric at the top and another at the bottom of the quilt. The quilting, which echoes the zigzags, can be created by hand or machine. This quilt requires no pattern pieces.

WHAT YOU NEED

FABRIC

FOR THE QUILT TOP

A total of 7 yards of cotton fabric, comprising the following (or your preferred) colors:

Deep Berry solid: 5⅔ yards for borders and triangles

Amaryllis Pink solid: ⅔ yard

Cassis Red solid: ⅔ yard

FOR THE QUILT BACK
Amaryllis Pink solid: 6¼ yards

FOR THE BINDING
Deep Berry solid: ¾ yard

OTHER MATERIALS
Cotton batting: 93 inches by 98 inches, for a queen-size quilt

(CONTINUED)

WHAT YOU DO

1 - Prepare the Top and Bottom Borders as follows: From the Deep Berry, cut two 87½-inch lengths. Trim off the selvage edges from both lengths. To create the Top Border, cut a 42½-inch-wide strip from one length. You will most likely use the full width of the fabric for the Top Border; just be sure to trim off the selvage edges. To create the Bottom Border, cut a 23¼-inch-wide strip from the second length.

2 - From the Amaryllis Pink, cut six squares, each 11 inches by 11 inches. Next, cut each of the squares in half diagonally to make twelve large triangles. Cut one triangle in half to make two small triangles (Figure 1). Set the triangles aside. Be aware that the long side of the triangle is cut on the bias of the fabric, which tends to stretch.

3 - Repeating Step 2, cut triangles from the Cassis Red. Set the triangles aside.

4 - From the Deep Berry, cut twelve 11-inch-by-11-inch squares. (You can cut about seven of these from the remnants of the fabric used to create the Bottom Border in Step 1.) Next, cut the twelve squares in half diagonally to make twenty-four large triangles. Cut two of these triangles in half to make four small triangles. Set aside.

5 - Arrange the zigzag rows in the "Ready-Set-Sew" position (see page 14). To create Row 1, lay out six large Cassis Red triangles and five large Deep Berry triangles, alternating colors as shown in Figure 4. Align the points where the seam lines intersect on each triangle (Figure 2), pin, then stitch the row together with a generous ¼-inch-wide seam allowance. Avoid pulling or tugging the triangles, as the long side is a bias cut, which tends to stretch. Press all seam allowances toward the Deep Berry.

6 - To create Row 2, repeat Step 5, however this time use six large Deep Berry triangles and five large Cassis Red ones. For Row 3, use six large Amaryllis Pink and five large Deep Berry triangles. For Row 4, use six large Deep Berry and five large Amaryllis Pink triangles.

7 - Pin and then stitch one small triangle to each end of each row. Use Deep Berry for Rows 1 and 3, Cassis Red for Row 2, and Amaryllis Pink for Row 4.

8 - Referring to "Stitch the Rows Together" on page 19 and with right sides together, pin and stitch Row 1 to Row 2. When pinning the rows together, center the triangle *points* of Row 1 on the *long sides* of the opposing triangle on Row 2, so your zigzags will be aligned. Be careful not to "cut off" the tips of the triangles when you sew the rows together. Repeat, pinning and then stitching Row 2 to Row 3, and then Row 3 to Row 4.

9 - With right sides together, stitch the Top Border to the top edge of Row 1 and the Bottom Border to the bottom edge of Row 4. Use the diagram as a guide, as necessary (Figure 4). Press.

10 - Referring to "Planning Your Quilting" and "Marking the Quilting Lines" on page 20, prepare your Quilt Top for quilting as follows: Using a fabric-marking pencil or dressmakers' chalk and an acrylic ruler, lightly mark vertical guidelines through the triangle points, and continue these lines through the Top and Bottom Borders. Using the zigzag lines created by the pieced triangles and the vertical lines as guides, mark a zigzag pattern every 1¼ inches, as shown (Figure 3).

11 - Using the methods described in "Constructing a Quilt" that begin on page 18, make a Quilt Back (see page 20), cut the batting (see page 20), then layer the Quilt Back, batting, and Quilt Top (see page 20). Baste the layers together by hand (see page 20) to create the quilt sandwich.

12 - If you plan to quilt by machine, refer to "Machine-Quilting" on page 23 to quilt as marked in Step 10. For hand-quilting, refer to the "Hand-Quilting Stitch" on page 21, to quilt as marked in Step 10.

13 - Square up your quilt (see page 29) to measure 87½ inches by 93 inches.

14 - Bind the quilt as described in "Binding the Quilt" on page 25.

FIGURE 1

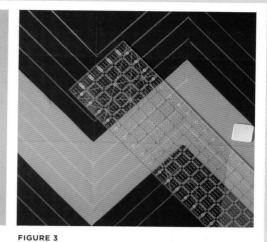

FIGURE 2

FIGURE 3

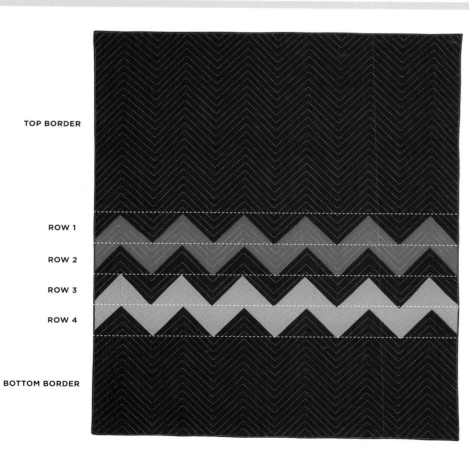

TOP BORDER

ROW 1

ROW 2

ROW 3

ROW 4

BOTTOM BORDER

FIGURE 4

PIE IN THE SKY

———

FINISHED SIZE: 65 INCHES BY 87 INCHES, FOR A TWIN-SIZE QUILT — BLOCK SIZE: 17 INCHES BY 17 INCHES
IF YOU'D LIKE TO MAKE THIS QUILT IN A DIFFERENT SIZE, CONSULT THE CHART IN "CHOOSING A QUILT SIZE" ON PAGE 18.

This quilt may be a bit more challenging than some of the other designs in this book, but making it is not a "pie-in-the-sky" goal. One pie pattern enlarged to three different sizes lends a subtle spin to the movement of this quilt. The pies are appliquéd onto individual blocks, which allows you to rotate each pie—so no two appear the same. Cut a few practice pies, and give it a whirl.

WHAT YOU NEED

Enlarge the "Pie in the Sky" patterns on page 163, as follows (see "Preparing the Pattern Pieces" on page 13). Clip out the notches on the pieces. Make sure you label each set of templates Small, Medium, and Large when you make the enlargements.

For the Small Pie, enlarge to 241 percent.
For the Medium Pie, enlarge to 250 percent.
For the Large Pie, enlarge to 265 percent.

FABRIC
FOR THE QUILT TOP
Slightly less than 8¼ yards of cotton fabric, comprising the following (or your preferred) colors:

Cocoa solid: ⅔ yard
Burnt Orange solid: 1¼ yards
Peacock Blue solid: 5 yards
Ecru solid: 1¼ yards

FOR THE QUILT BACK
A total of 4½ yards of cotton fabric, comprising the following (or your preferred) colors:

Burnt Orange solid: 2 yards
Peacock Blue solid: 2 yards
Orange print: ½ yard

FOR THE BINDING
Orange print: ½ yard

OTHER MATERIALS
Cotton batting: 70 inches by 93 inches, for a twin-size quilt

(CONTINUED)

ANATOMY OF A PIE

Think of the A and B pieces as the Pie Filling and the C pieces as the Pie Crust.

WHAT YOU DO

1 - Referring to "Laying Out and Cutting" on page 13, cut out the Background Blocks and Border pieces as follows, then set them aside.

FOR THE BACKGROUND BLOCKS
Cut twelve 17½-inch-by-17½-inch Peacock Blue squares.

FOR TOP AND BOTTOM BORDERS
Cut three 10-inch-wide Peacock Blue strips selvage to selvage.

FOR LEFT AND RIGHT BORDER
Cut five 7½-inch-wide Peacock Blue strips selvage to selvage.

2 - Lay out the Quilt Top templates on the right sides of the fabrics. Trace the templates and cut out the pieces as follows.

FOR THE SMALL PIE
For A pieces: Cut three Cocoa.
For B pieces: Cut three Burnt Orange.
For C pieces: Cut twelve Ecru.

FOR THE MEDIUM PIE
For A pieces: Cut four Cocoa.
For B pieces: Cut four Burnt Orange.
For C pieces: Cut sixteen Ecru.

FOR THE LARGE PIE
For A pieces: Cut five Cocoa.
For B pieces: Cut five Burnt Orange.
For C pieces: Cut twenty Ecru.

3 - Transfer the notches on the B-1, B-3, B-4, and B-6 templates to the corresponding fabric pieces. Arrange the A and B pieces in the "Ready-Set-Sew" position (see page 14).

4 - Using the "String-Piecing Method" on page 16, with right sides together, stitch the Small Pie pieces together in the following order: Stitch B-1 to A-1, then A-1 to B-2. Stitch this unit to A-2, then A-2 to B-3 and B-3 to A-3, then A-3 to B-4. This completes the bottom half of the pie (Figure 1). *Note: Since the outer edges of the pies are curved, the edges won't quite line up when you place them right sides together. For this reason, align the points where the seam lines intersect on each piece (Figure 2). Set the stitched pieces aside.*

5 - To complete the top half of the Pie, with right sides together, stitch the Pie pieces together in the following order: B-7 to A-5, then A-5 to B-6, B-6 to A-4, and A-4 to B-5.

6 - With right sides together, stitch the bottom half of the Small Pie to A-Center and A-Center to the top half of the Small Pie (Figure 3).

7 - With right sides together, stitch four pieces of C together to make the Pie Crust (Figure 4).

8 - With right sides together, match the seams on the Pie Crust to the notch marks on the Pie, and pin. Align the Pie and Crust edges, easing the Crust fullness, and pin (Figure 5). Stitch, and then press the seam allowance toward the Pie Crust.

9 - Repeat Steps 4 through 8 for the Medium and Large Pies.

10 - Referring to "Appliqué" on page 27, prepare the pies for appliqué by lightly penciling a line 3/16 inch from the outside edge around each of the Pie Crusts. Position each Pie on a Background Block, making sure to rotate them at various angles so they will all look different in the finished quilt. You can also position some slightly off center. Hand-baste each pie to the Background Block (Figure 6). With a blind stitch (see page 27), appliqué each pie to the Background Block (Figure 7).

(CONTINUED)

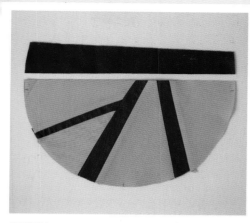

FIGURE 1

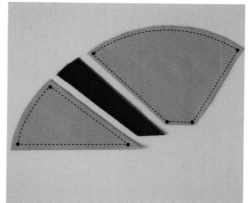

FIGURE 2

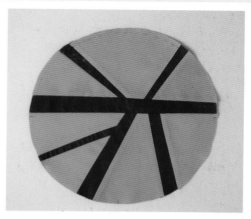

FIGURE 3

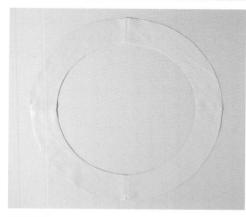

FIGURE 4

FIGURE 5

FIGURE 6

FIGURE 7

11 - Referring to "Arrange the Quilt Blocks" on page 19, arrange the appliquéd blocks on your design wall or the floor. Use Figure 8 as a guide or produce your own design. Vary the placement of Pie sizes and rotations for variety and movement.

12 - When you are happy with your arrangement, refer to "Move 'Em to the Machine" on page 19, and remove the blocks from the design wall or floor. Referring to "Blocks into Rows" and "Stitch the Rows Together" (see page 19), stitch the blocks together, and press.

13 - With right sides together and placed end to end, stitch together the three Top and Bottom Border strips to make one long strip. From this long strip, cut two 65-inch-long pieces for the Top and Bottom Borders. With right sides together and placed end to end, stitch together the four Side Border strips to make one long strip. From this long strip, cut two 88-inch-long strips for the Left and Right Borders.

14 - With right sides together, stitch the Top and Bottom Borders to the top and bottom edges of the Quilt Top, then stitch the Left and Right Borders to the side edges of the Quilt Top.

15 - Referring to "Planning Your Quilting" and "Marking the Quilting Lines" on page 20, prepare your Quilt Top for hand-quilting. First, create a diagonal guideline. Run a taut length of string diagonally from the top left-hand corner to the bottom right-hand corner. With a fabric-marking pencil or dressmakers' chalk and an acrylic ruler, use the string as a guide to mark parallel diagonal lines every $1\frac{1}{4}$ inches, skipping over the Pies. Continue to mark parallel diagonal lines until you reach the corners.

16 - Next, mark a series of concentric circles every $1\frac{1}{4}$ inch, working from the outside to the inside of each Pie. Don't bother to mark the inner and outer circumferences of the Pie Crust, as these will be quilted using the stitch-in-the-ditch method.

17 - Using the methods described in "Constructing a Quilt" that begin on page 18, make a Quilt Back (see page 20), cut the batting (see page 20), then layer the Quilt Back, batting, and Quilt Top (see page 20). Baste the layers together by hand (see page 20) to create the quilt sandwich.

18 - Referring to the "Hand-Quilting Stitch" on page 21, quilt the diagonal lines, starting with the centermost line and work toward the outside edges of the quilt. Refer to "Stitch-in-the-Ditch Quilting" on page 20 to stitch around the outer and inner circumferences of the Pie Crusts. Then, quilt the marked inner circles.

19 - Square up your quilt (see page 29) to measure 65 inches by 87 inches.

20 - Bind the quilt as described in "Binding the Quilt" on page 25.

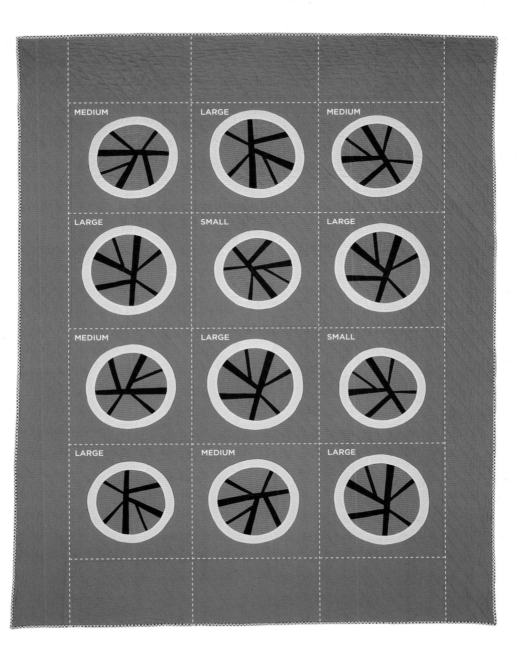

FIGURE 8

TEN QUILTS · **149**

DRUNK LOVE 2-TONE

FINISHED SIZE: 78 INCHES BY 86 INCHES, FOR A FULL-SIZE QUILT — FINISHED BLOCK SIZE: 13 INCHES BY 13 INCHES
IF YOU'D LIKE TO MAKE THIS QUILT IN A DIFFERENT SIZE, CONSULT THE CHART IN "CHOOSING A QUILT SIZE" ON PAGE 18.

Only three bicolor block patterns are used to create this eye-catching quilt. The secret to its animated appearance is in the color arrangement. Each of the block patterns is created in two ways: one with the deepest color at the center and the other with the lighter color at the center. One of the most popular designs in the Denyse Schmidt Quilts collection, this quilt can be created with any two solid colors that are similar in hue. For more subtle results, choose two colors that are close in value. For a more active design, choose two colors with a greater value-difference.

WHAT YOU NEED

Enlarge the "Drunk Love 2-Tone" patterns on pages 168–170 to 400 percent (see "Preparing the Pattern Pieces" on page 13).

FABRIC
FOR THE QUILT TOP
A total of 8⅔ yards of cotton fabric, comprising the following (or your preferred) colors:

Taxi Cab Yellow solid: 4⅔ yards
School Bus Orange solid: 4 yards

FOR THE QUILT BACK
Truck Turquoise solid: 5½ yards

FOR THE BINDING
Taxi Cab Yellow solid: ¾ yard

OTHER MATERIALS
Cotton batting: 84 inches by 91 inches, for a full-size quilt

2-TONE TIMING

This is among the more challenging quilts in this book, as each block is composed of several pattern pieces, all of which look deceptively similar. For best results, stitch only one block at a time—and don't rush through the project.

(CONTINUED)

WHAT YOU DO

1 - Begin by cutting your Top and Bottom Border pieces: Cut five Taxi Cab Yellow strips, each 4¼ inches wide selvage to selvage. Set aside.

2 - Use the following time-saving process to prepare the fabric for cutting out your block pieces: From the Taxi Cab Yellow, cut nine 16-inch-wide lengths selvage to selvage (see "Cutting Selvage to Selvage" on page 13). Next, cut each of the nine Yellow lengths in half *widthwise*, along the fold, so you end up with eighteen Yellow rectangles, each measuring about 16 inches by 21 inches. Repeat with the School Bus Orange fabric. You will now have eighteen Orange rectangles and eighteen Yellow rectangles. Create three groups of rectangles (one group for each of the three block patterns), each with six Orange and six Yellow rectangles. Set the groups for Block 2 and Block 3 aside.

3 - For Block 1, make three stacks of four rectangles each, with *alternating* colors. Each stack should have an Orange rectangle on top.

4 - Referring to "Laying Out and Cutting" on page 13, lay out, trace, and cut all Block 1 pieces from the first stack. Arrange them in the "Ready-Set-Sew" position (see page 14). Repeat with the other two stacks, arranging all pieces in Ready-Set-Sew on top of the pieces from the first stack of fabric. You will now have twelve layers of each Block 1 piece, with the colors alternating from layer to layer (Figure 1).

5 - Shuffle the Block 1 Center from the top layer to the bottom of the stack (Figure 2). Next, shuffle each of the B pieces from the top layer to the bottom of the stack (Figure 3). Then, shuffle each of the D pieces from the top layer to the bottom of the stack. Block 1 is now positioned in the Ready-Set-Sew position, with alternating colors in each frame (Figure 4). You may not appreciate the beauty of this process until you start sewing the blocks together, but it spares you the time-consuming task of laying out every block in Ready-Set-Sew with alternating frame colors!

6 - Using a "Compass Pin" (see page 15) and referring to the "Modified–Log Cabin Method" on page 15, with right sides together, stitch all Block 1 pieces together. As you stitch each layer of blocks together, the colors will reverse, but still alternate for each frame of each block. Press.

7 - Square up (see page 29) each block to measure 13½ inches by 13½ inches. Set aside.

8 - Repeat Steps 2 through 7 for Blocks 2 and 3.

9 - Referring to "Arrange the Quilt Blocks" on page 19, arrange the blocks on your design wall or floor. Refer to Figure 5 or produce a design of your own. Some of the blocks have more of one color or the other, so arrange the blocks with an eye toward balancing the color placement. Rotate a few of the blocks to make the design look less predictable.

10 - When you are pleased with the arrangement, refer to "Move 'Em to the Machine" on page 19, and remove the blocks from the design wall or floor. Referring to "Blocks into Rows" and "Stitch the Rows Together" (see page 19), stitch the quilt blocks together, and press.

11 - With right sides together and placed end to end, stitch the Top and Bottom Border strips together to make one long strip. Cut this strip into two 78½-inch-long Top and Bottom Borders. With right sides together, stitch the Top and Bottom Borders to the top and bottom edges of the Quilt Top.

12 - Referring to "Planning Your Quilting" and "Marking the Quilting Lines" on page 20, prepare your Quilt Top for hand-quilting. We quilted by stitching-in-the-ditch, following the concentric square-in-a-square design. You don't need to mark for stitch-in-the-ditch quilting, but use a fabric-marking pencil or dressmakers' chalk and an acrylic ruler to mark one or two additional concentric squares inside a few of the squares for added variety. (We quilted additional squares in the Block 3 Centers and in some of the wider pieces of Block 2.) Your marked quilting lines don't need to be identical in placement. In fact, varying them by marking some closer to the seam lines and others farther away will yield more interesting results. Next, mark two quilting lines along the border strips, one parallel to and 1¼ inches from the seam, and the other parallel to and 1¼ inches from the first line.

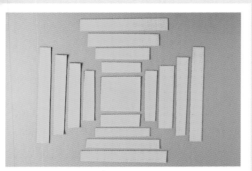

FIGURE 1

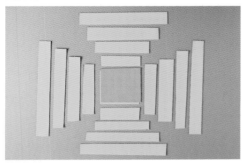

FIGURE 2

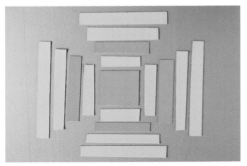

FIGURE 3

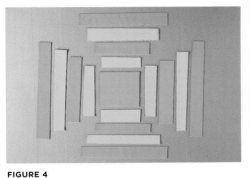

FIGURE 4

13 - Using the methods described in "Constructing a Quilt" that begin on page 18, make a Quilt Back (see page 20), cut the batting (see page 20), then layer the Quilt Back, batting, and Quilt Top (see page 20). Baste the layers together by hand (see page 20) to create the quilt sandwich.

14 - Referring to the "Hand-Quilting Stitch" on page 21, stitch on the quilting lines you marked in Step 12 and stitch-in-the-ditch.

15 - Square up your quilt (see page 29) to measure 78 inches by 86 inches.

16 - Bind the quilt as described in "Binding the Quilt" on page 25.

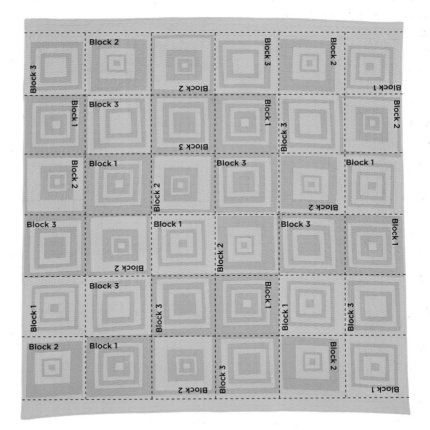

FIGURE 5

PATTERNS

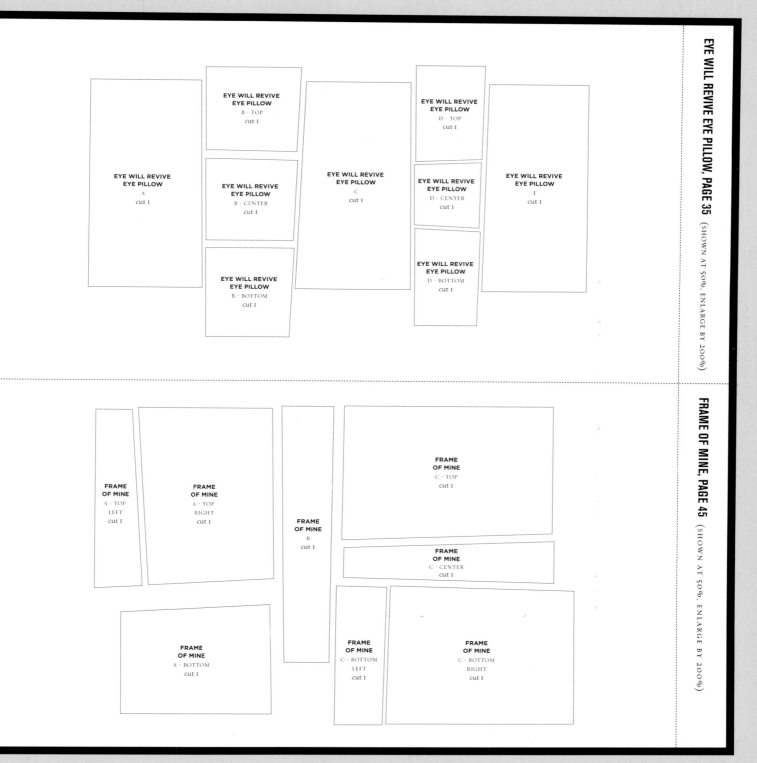

EYE WILL REVIVE
EYE PILLOW
B - TOP
cut I

EYE WILL REVIVE
EYE PILLOW
D - TOP
cut I

EYE WILL REVIVE
EYE PILLOW
A
cut I

EYE WILL REVIVE
EYE PILLOW
B - CENTER
cut I

EYE WILL REVIVE
EYE PILLOW
C
cut I

EYE WILL REVIVE
EYE PILLOW
D - CENTER
cut I

EYE WILL REVIVE
EYE PILLOW
E
cut I

EYE WILL REVIVE
EYE PILLOW
B - BOTTOM
cut I

EYE WILL REVIVE
EYE PILLOW
D - BOTTOM
cut I

FRAME
OF MINE
A - TOP
LEFT
cut I

FRAME
OF MINE
A - TOP
RIGHT
cut I

FRAME
OF MINE
B
cut I

FRAME
OF MINE
C - TOP
cut I

FRAME
OF MINE
C - CENTER
cut I

FRAME
OF MINE
A - BOTTOM
cut I

FRAME
OF MINE
C - BOTTOM
LEFT
cut I

FRAME
OF MINE
C - BOTTOM
RIGHT
cut I

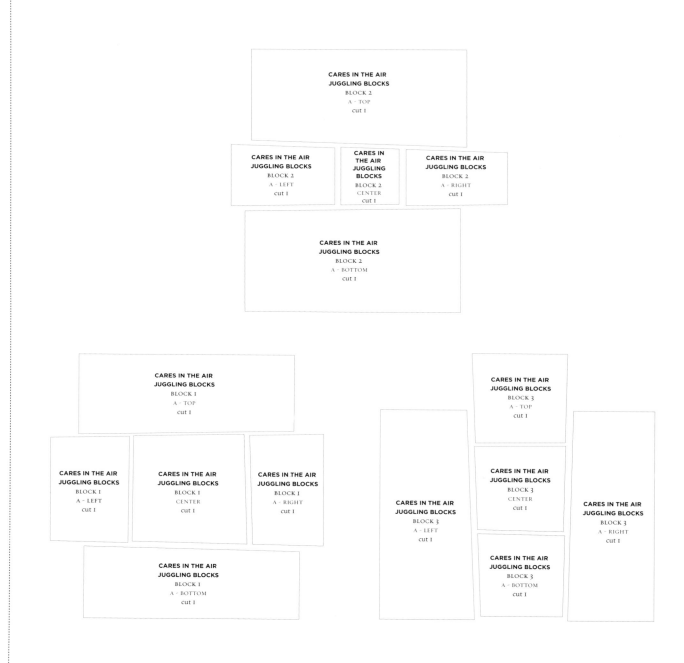

CARES IN THE AIR
JUGGLING BLOCKS
BLOCK 2
A - TOP
cut I

CARES IN THE AIR
JUGGLING BLOCKS
BLOCK 2
A - LEFT
cut I

CARES IN
THE AIR
JUGGLING
BLOCKS
BLOCK 2
CENTER
cut I

CARES IN THE AIR
JUGGLING BLOCKS
BLOCK 2
A - RIGHT
cut I

CARES IN THE AIR
JUGGLING BLOCKS
BLOCK 2
A - BOTTOM
cut I

CARES IN THE AIR
JUGGLING BLOCKS
BLOCK I
A - TOP
cut I

CARES IN THE AIR
JUGGLING BLOCKS
BLOCK 3
A - TOP
cut I

CARES IN THE AIR
JUGGLING BLOCKS
BLOCK I
A - LEFT
cut I

CARES IN THE AIR
JUGGLING BLOCKS
BLOCK I
CENTER
cut I

CARES IN THE AIR
JUGGLING BLOCKS
BLOCK I
A - RIGHT
cut I

CARES IN THE AIR
JUGGLING BLOCKS
BLOCK 3
A - LEFT
cut I

CARES IN THE AIR
JUGGLING BLOCKS
BLOCK 3
CENTER
cut I

CARES IN THE AIR
JUGGLING BLOCKS
BLOCK 3
A - RIGHT
cut I

CARES IN THE AIR
JUGGLING BLOCKS
BLOCK I
A - BOTTOM
cut I

CARES IN THE AIR
JUGGLING BLOCKS
BLOCK 3
A - BOTTOM
cut I

MIX-IT-UP COCKTAIL COASTERS, PAGE 65 (SHOWN AT 50%, ENLARGE BY 200%)

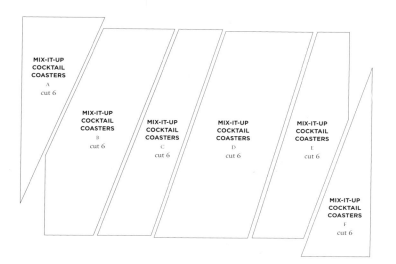

MIX-IT-UP COCKTAIL COASTERS
A
cut 6

MIX-IT-UP COCKTAIL COASTERS
B
cut 6

MIX-IT-UP COCKTAIL COASTERS
C
cut 6

MIX-IT-UP COCKTAIL COASTERS
D
cut 6

MIX-IT-UP COCKTAIL COASTERS
E
cut 6

MIX-IT-UP COCKTAIL COASTERS
F
cut 6

CLOSET CASE SACHET, PAGE 97 (SHOWN AT 50%, ENLARGE BY 200%)

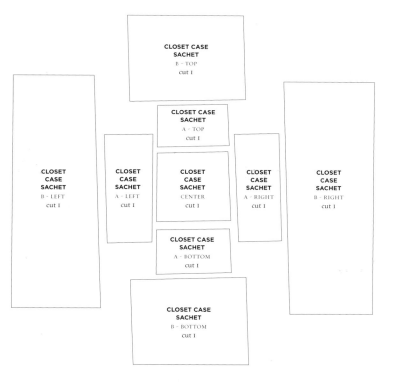

CLOSET CASE SACHET
B – TOP
cut 1

CLOSET CASE SACHET
A – TOP
cut 1

CLOSET CASE SACHET
B – LEFT
cut 1

CLOSET CASE SACHET
A – LEFT
cut 1

CLOSET CASE SACHET
CENTER
cut 1

CLOSET CASE SACHET
A – RIGHT
cut 1

CLOSET CASE SACHET
B – RIGHT
cut 1

CLOSET CASE SACHET
A – BOTTOM
cut 1

CLOSET CASE SACHET
B – BOTTOM
cut 1

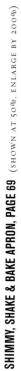

**SHIMMY, SHAKE
& BAKE APRON**
POCKET
C - TOP
cut I

**SHIMMY, SHAKE
& BAKE APRON**
POCKET
C - LEFT I
cut I

**SHIMMY, SHAKE
& BAKE APRON**
POCKET
B - TOP
cut I

**SHIMMY, SHAKE
& BAKE APRON**
POCKET
C - RIGHT
cut I

**SHIMMY, SHAKE
& BAKE APRON**
POCKET
A - TOP - cut I

**SHIMMY,
SHAKE
& BAKE
APRON**
POCKET
A - LEFT
cut I

**SHIMMY, SHAKE
& BAKE APRON**
POCKET
CENTER
cut I

**SHIMMY,
SHAKE
& BAKE
APRON**
POCKET
A - RIGHT
cut I

**SHIMMY, SHAKE
& BAKE APRON**
POCKET
B - RIGHT
cut I

**SHIMMY, SHAKE
& BAKE APRON**
POCKET
B - LEFT
cut I

**SHIMMY, SHAKE
& BAKE APRON**
POCKET
A - BOTTOM - cut I

**SHIMMY, SHAKE
& BAKE APRON**
POCKET
C - LEFT 2
cut I

**SHIMMY, SHAKE
& BAKE APRON**
POCKET
B - BOTTOM
cut I

**SHIMMY, SHAKE
& BAKE APRON**
POCKET
C - BOTTOM
cut I

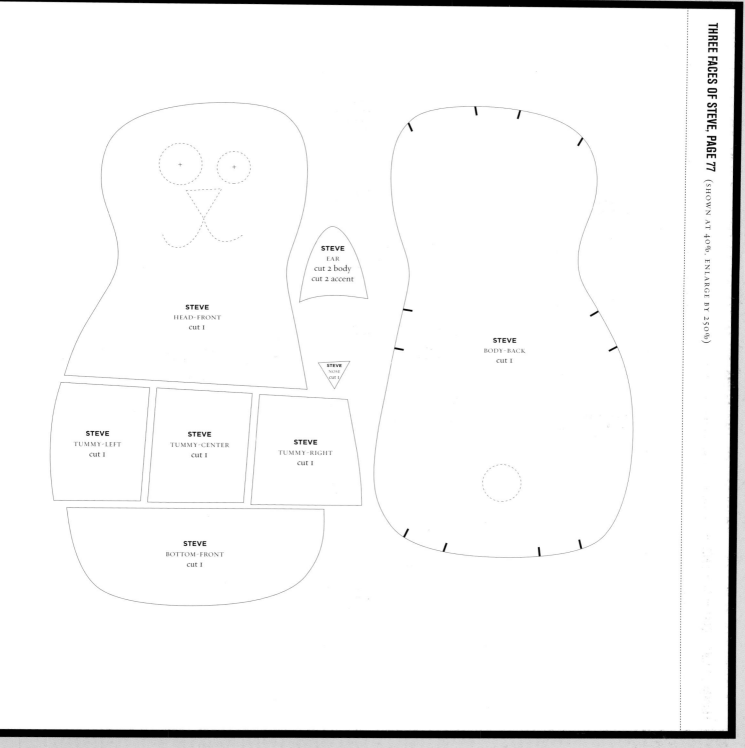

STEVE
HEAD-FRONT
cut 1

STEVE
EAR
cut 2 body
cut 2 accent

STEVE
NOSE
cut 1

STEVE
TUMMY-LEFT
cut 1

STEVE
TUMMY-CENTER
cut 1

STEVE
TUMMY-RIGHT
cut 1

STEVE
BOTTOM-FRONT
cut 1

STEVE
BODY-BACK
cut 1

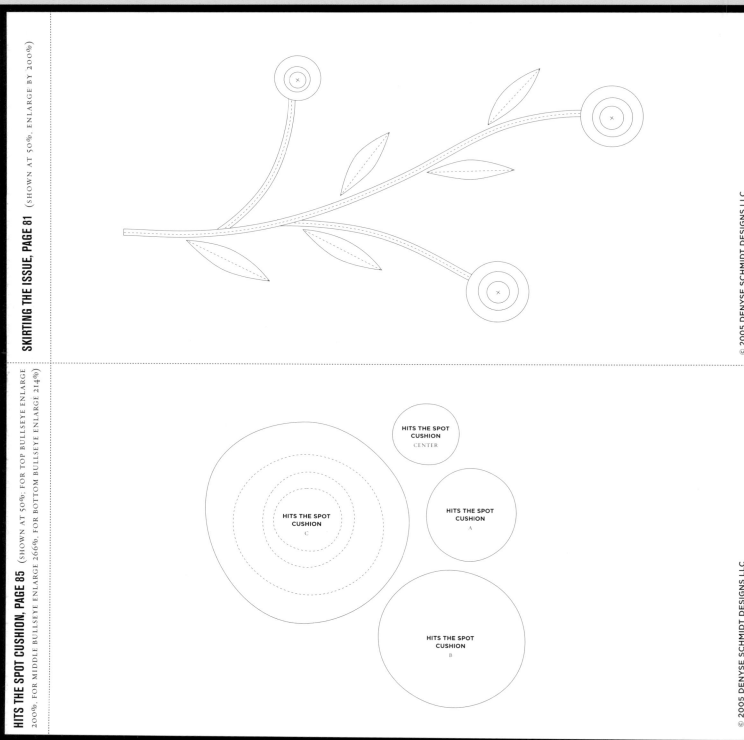

SKIRTING THE ISSUE, PAGE 81 (SHOWN AT 50%, ENLARGE BY 200%)

HITS THE SPOT CUSHION, PAGE 85 (SHOWN AT 50%; FOR TOP BULLSEYE ENLARGE 200%, FOR MIDDLE BULLSEYE ENLARGE 266%, FOR BOTTOM BULLSEYE ENLARGE 214%)

HITS THE SPOT CUSHION
CENTER

HITS THE SPOT CUSHION
C

HITS THE SPOT CUSHION
A

HITS THE SPOT CUSHION
B

HOLD ME CLOSE
HEATING PAD COVER
D - TOP
cut I

HOLD ME CLOSE HEATING PAD COVER
C - TOP - cut I

HOLD ME CLOSE
HEATING PAD COVER
B - TOP - cut I

HOLD ME CLOSE
HEATING PAD COVER
A - TOP - cut I

HOLD ME CLOSE
HEATING PAD COVER
CENTER - cut I

HOLD ME CLOSE HEATING PAD COVER
D - LEFT cut I

HOLD ME CLOSE HEATING PAD COVER
C - LEFT cut I

HOLD ME CLOSE HEATING PAD COVER
B - LEFT cut I

HOLD ME CLOSE HEATING PAD COVER
A - LEFT cut I

HOLD ME CLOSE HEATING PAD COVER
A - RIGHT cut I

HOLD ME CLOSE HEATING PAD COVER
B - RIGHT cut I

HOLD ME CLOSE HEATING PAD COVER
C - RIGHT cut I

HOLD ME CLOSE HEATING PAD COVER
D - RIGHT cut I

HOLD ME CLOSE
HEATING PAD COVER
A - BOTTOM - cut I

HOLD ME CLOSE
HEATING PAD COVER
B - BOTTOM - cut I

HOLD ME CLOSE HEATING PAD COVER
C - BOTTOM - cut I

HOLD ME CLOSE HEATING PAD COVER
D - BOTTOM - cut I

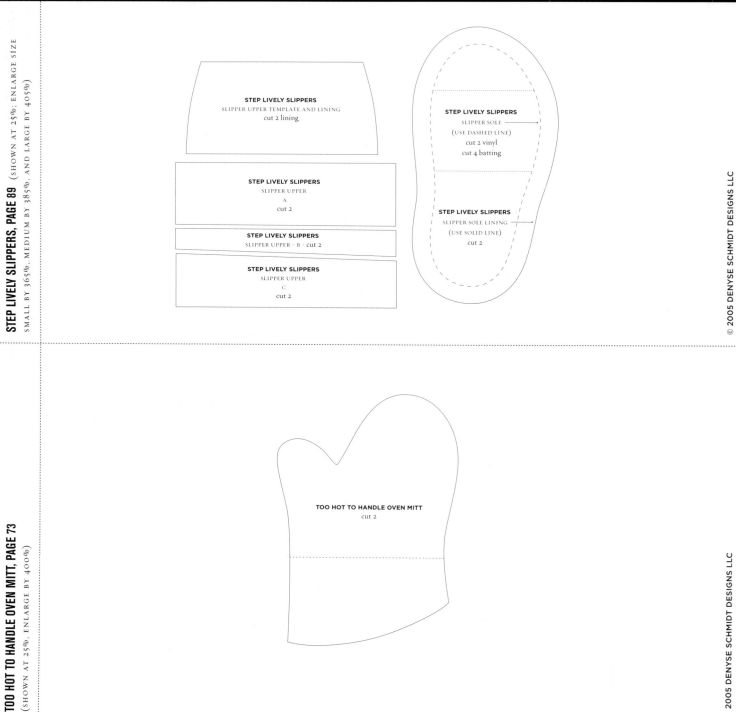

STEP LIVELY SLIPPERS
SLIPPER UPPER TEMPLATE AND LINING
cut 2 lining

STEP LIVELY SLIPPERS
SLIPPER UPPER
A
cut 2

STEP LIVELY SLIPPERS
SLIPPER UPPER - B - cut 2

STEP LIVELY SLIPPERS
SLIPPER UPPER
C
cut 2

STEP LIVELY SLIPPERS
SLIPPER SOLE
(USE DASHED LINE)
cut 2 vinyl
cut 4 batting

STEP LIVELY SLIPPERS
SLIPPER SOLE LINING
(USE SOLID LINE)
cut 2

TOO HOT TO HANDLE OVEN MITT
cut 2

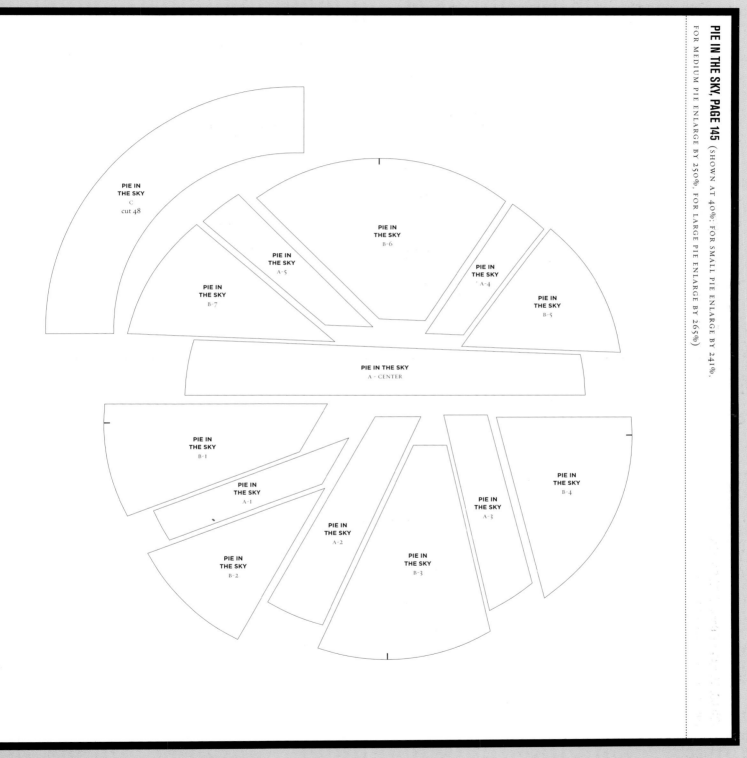

PIE IN THE SKY, PAGE 145 (SHOWN AT 40%; FOR SMALL PIE ENLARGE BY 241%;
FOR MEDIUM PIE ENLARGE BY 250%; FOR LARGE PIE ENLARGE BY 265%)

PIE IN
THE SKY
C
cut 48

PIE IN
THE SKY
B-6

PIE IN
THE SKY
A-5

PIE IN
THE SKY
B-7

PIE IN
THE SKY
A-4

PIE IN
THE SKY
B-5

PIE IN THE SKY
A – CENTER

PIE IN
THE SKY
B-1

PIE IN
THE SKY
A-1

PIE IN
THE SKY
A-2

PIE IN
THE SKY
B-2

PIE IN
THE SKY
B-3

PIE IN
THE SKY
A-3

PIE IN
THE SKY
B-4

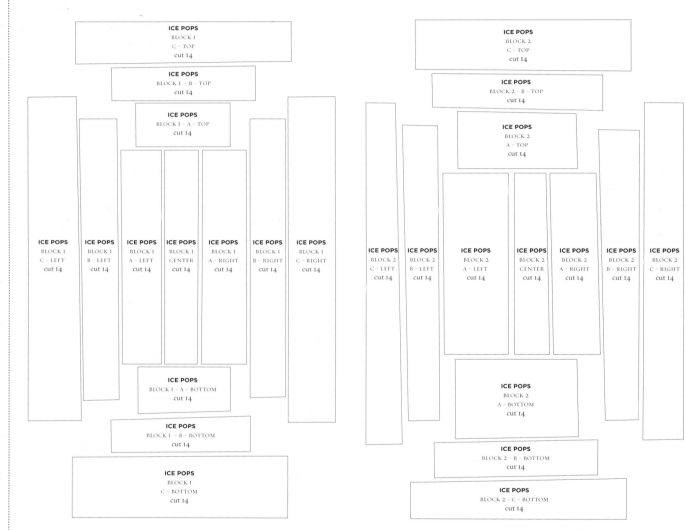

ICE POPS
BLOCK I
C - TOP
cut 14

ICE POPS
BLOCK 2
C - TOP
cut 14

ICE POPS
BLOCK I - B - TOP
cut 14

ICE POPS
BLOCK 2 - B - TOP
cut 14

ICE POPS
BLOCK I - A - TOP
cut 14

ICE POPS
BLOCK 2
A - TOP
cut 14

ICE POPS
BLOCK I
C - LEFT
cut 14

ICE POPS
BLOCK I
B - LEFT
cut 14

ICE POPS
BLOCK I
A - LEFT
cut 14

ICE POPS
BLOCK I
CENTER
cut 14

ICE POPS
BLOCK I
A - RIGHT
cut 14

ICE POPS
BLOCK I
B - RIGHT
cut 14

ICE POPS
BLOCK I
C - RIGHT
cut 14

ICE POPS
BLOCK 2
C - LEFT
cut 14

ICE POPS
BLOCK 2
B - LEFT
cut 14

ICE POPS
BLOCK 2
A - LEFT
cut 14

ICE POPS
BLOCK 2
CENTER
cut 14

ICE POPS
BLOCK 2
A - RIGHT
cut 14

ICE POPS
BLOCK 2
B - RIGHT
cut 14

ICE POPS
BLOCK 2
C - RIGHT
cut 14

ICE POPS
BLOCK I - A - BOTTOM
cut 14

ICE POPS
BLOCK 2
A - BOTTOM
cut 14

ICE POPS
BLOCK I - B - BOTTOM
cut 14

ICE POPS
BLOCK 2 - B - BOTTOM
cut 14

ICE POPS
BLOCK I
C - BOTTOM
cut 14

ICE POPS
BLOCK 2 - C - BOTTOM
cut 14

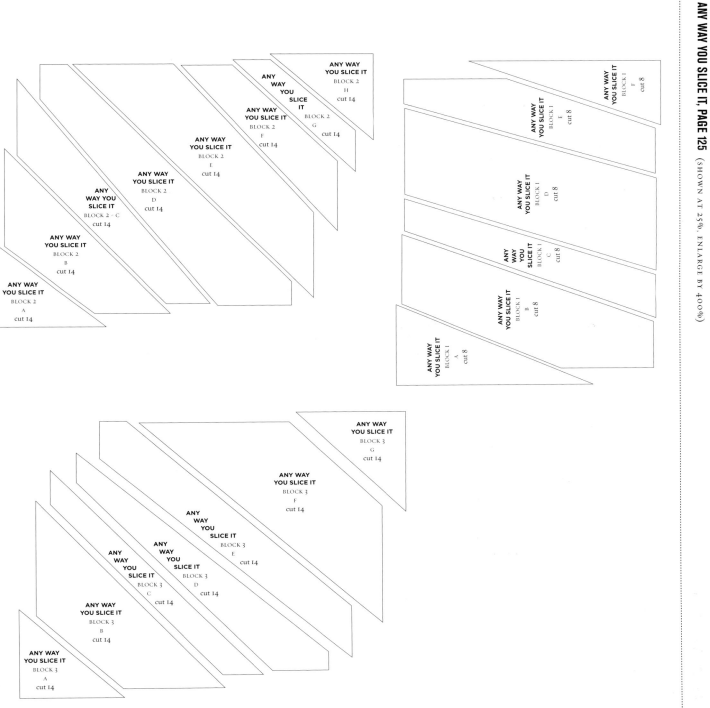

ANY WAY YOU SLICE IT
BLOCK 1
F
cut 8

ANY WAY YOU SLICE IT
BLOCK 1
E
cut 8

ANY WAY YOU SLICE IT
BLOCK 1
D
cut 8

ANY WAY YOU SLICE IT
BLOCK 1
C
cut 8

ANY WAY YOU SLICE IT
BLOCK 1
B
cut 8

ANY WAY YOU SLICE IT
BLOCK 1
A
cut 8

ANY WAY YOU SLICE IT
BLOCK 2
H
cut 14

ANY WAY YOU SLICE IT
BLOCK 2
G
cut 14

ANY WAY YOU SLICE IT
BLOCK 2
F
cut 14

ANY WAY YOU SLICE IT
BLOCK 2
E
cut 14

ANY WAY YOU SLICE IT
BLOCK 2
D
cut 14

ANY WAY YOU SLICE IT
BLOCK 2 - C
cut 14

ANY WAY YOU SLICE IT
BLOCK 2
B
cut 14

ANY WAY YOU SLICE IT
BLOCK 2
A
cut 14

ANY WAY YOU SLICE IT
BLOCK 3
G
cut 14

ANY WAY YOU SLICE IT
BLOCK 3
F
cut 14

ANY WAY YOU SLICE IT
BLOCK 3
E
cut 14

ANY WAY YOU SLICE IT
BLOCK 3
D
cut 14

ANY WAY YOU SLICE IT
BLOCK 3
C
cut 14

ANY WAY YOU SLICE IT
BLOCK 3
B
cut 14

ANY WAY YOU SLICE IT
BLOCK 3
A
cut 14

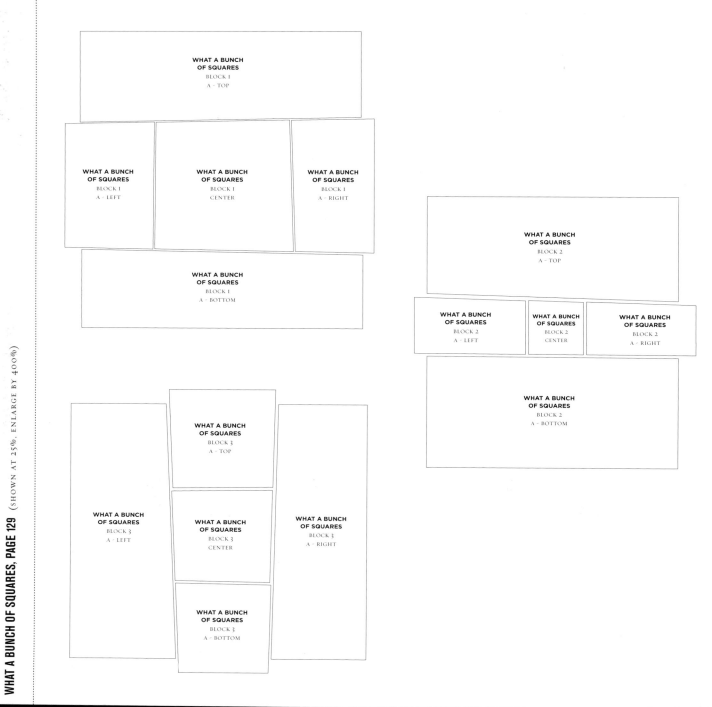

WHAT A BUNCH
OF SQUARES
BLOCK 1
A - TOP

WHAT A BUNCH
OF SQUARES
BLOCK 1
A - LEFT

WHAT A BUNCH
OF SQUARES
BLOCK 1
CENTER

WHAT A BUNCH
OF SQUARES
BLOCK 1
A - RIGHT

WHAT A BUNCH
OF SQUARES
BLOCK 1
A - BOTTOM

WHAT A BUNCH
OF SQUARES
BLOCK 2
A - TOP

WHAT A BUNCH
OF SQUARES
BLOCK 2
A - LEFT

WHAT A BUNCH
OF SQUARES
BLOCK 2
CENTER

WHAT A BUNCH
OF SQUARES
BLOCK 2
A - RIGHT

WHAT A BUNCH
OF SQUARES
BLOCK 2
A - BOTTOM

WHAT A BUNCH
OF SQUARES
BLOCK 3
A - TOP

WHAT A BUNCH
OF SQUARES
BLOCK 3
A - LEFT

WHAT A BUNCH
OF SQUARES
BLOCK 3
CENTER

WHAT A BUNCH
OF SQUARES
BLOCK 3
A - RIGHT

WHAT A BUNCH
OF SQUARES
BLOCK 3
A - BOTTOM

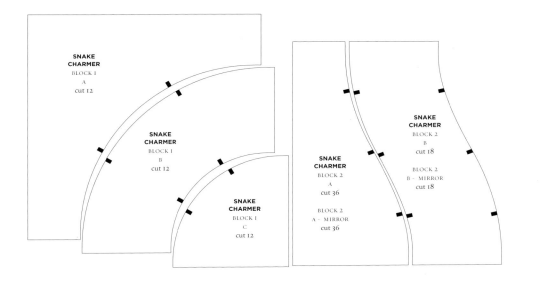

SNAKE CHARMER
BLOCK 1
A
cut 12

SNAKE CHARMER
BLOCK 1
B
cut 12

SNAKE CHARMER
BLOCK 1
C
cut 12

SNAKE CHARMER
BLOCK 2
A
cut 36

BLOCK 2
A - MIRROR
cut 36

SNAKE CHARMER
BLOCK 2
B
cut 18

BLOCK 2
B - MIRROR
cut 18

HOP, SKIP & A JUMP
A
cut 7 muslin
cut 5 red

HOP, SKIP & A JUMP
B
cut 5 muslin
cut 7 red

HOP, SKIP & A JUMP
C
cut 7 muslin
cut 5 red

HOP, SKIP & A JUMP
D
cut 5 muslin
cut 7 red

HOP, SKIP & A JUMP
E
cut 7 muslin
cut 5 red

HOP, SKIP & A JUMP
F
cut 5 muslin
cut 7 red

HOP, SKIP & A JUMP
G
cut 7 muslin
cut 5 red

HOP, SKIP & A JUMP
H
cut 5 muslin
cut 7 red

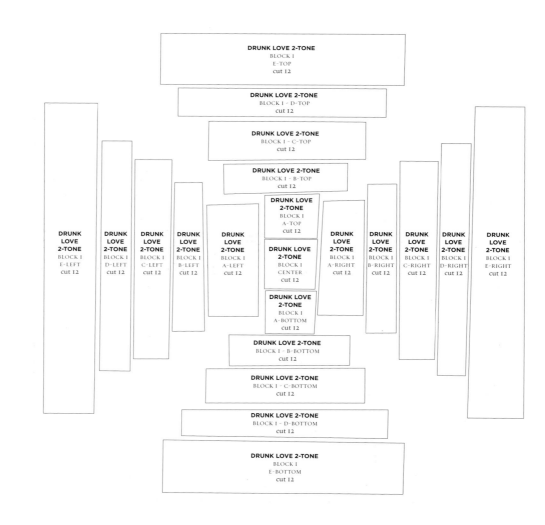

DRUNK LOVE 2-TONE
BLOCK I
E-TOP
cut 12

DRUNK LOVE 2-TONE
BLOCK I - D-TOP
cut 12

DRUNK LOVE 2-TONE
BLOCK I - C-TOP
cut 12

DRUNK LOVE 2-TONE
BLOCK I - B-TOP
cut 12

DRUNK LOVE
2-TONE
BLOCK I
A-TOP
cut 12

DRUNK LOVE
2-TONE
BLOCK I
E-LEFT
cut 12

DRUNK
LOVE
2-TONE
BLOCK I
D-LEFT
cut 12

DRUNK
LOVE
2-TONE
BLOCK I
C-LEFT
cut 12

DRUNK
LOVE
2-TONE
BLOCK I
B-LEFT
cut 12

DRUNK
LOVE
2-TONE
BLOCK I
A-LEFT
cut 12

DRUNK LOVE
2-TONE
BLOCK I
CENTER
cut 12

DRUNK
LOVE
2-TONE
BLOCK I
A-RIGHT
cut 12

DRUNK
LOVE
2-TONE
BLOCK I
B-RIGHT
cut 12

DRUNK
LOVE
2-TONE
BLOCK I
C-RIGHT
cut 12

DRUNK
LOVE
2-TONE
BLOCK I
D-RIGHT
cut 12

DRUNK
LOVE
2-TONE
BLOCK I
E-RIGHT
cut 12

DRUNK LOVE
2-TONE
BLOCK I
A-BOTTOM
cut 12

DRUNK LOVE 2-TONE
BLOCK I - B-BOTTOM
cut 12

DRUNK LOVE 2-TONE
BLOCK I - C-BOTTOM
cut 12

DRUNK LOVE 2-TONE
BLOCK I - D-BOTTOM
cut 12

DRUNK LOVE 2-TONE
BLOCK I
E-BOTTOM
cut 12

DRUNK LOVE 2-TONE, PAGE 151 (SHOWN AT 25%, ENLARGE BY 400%)

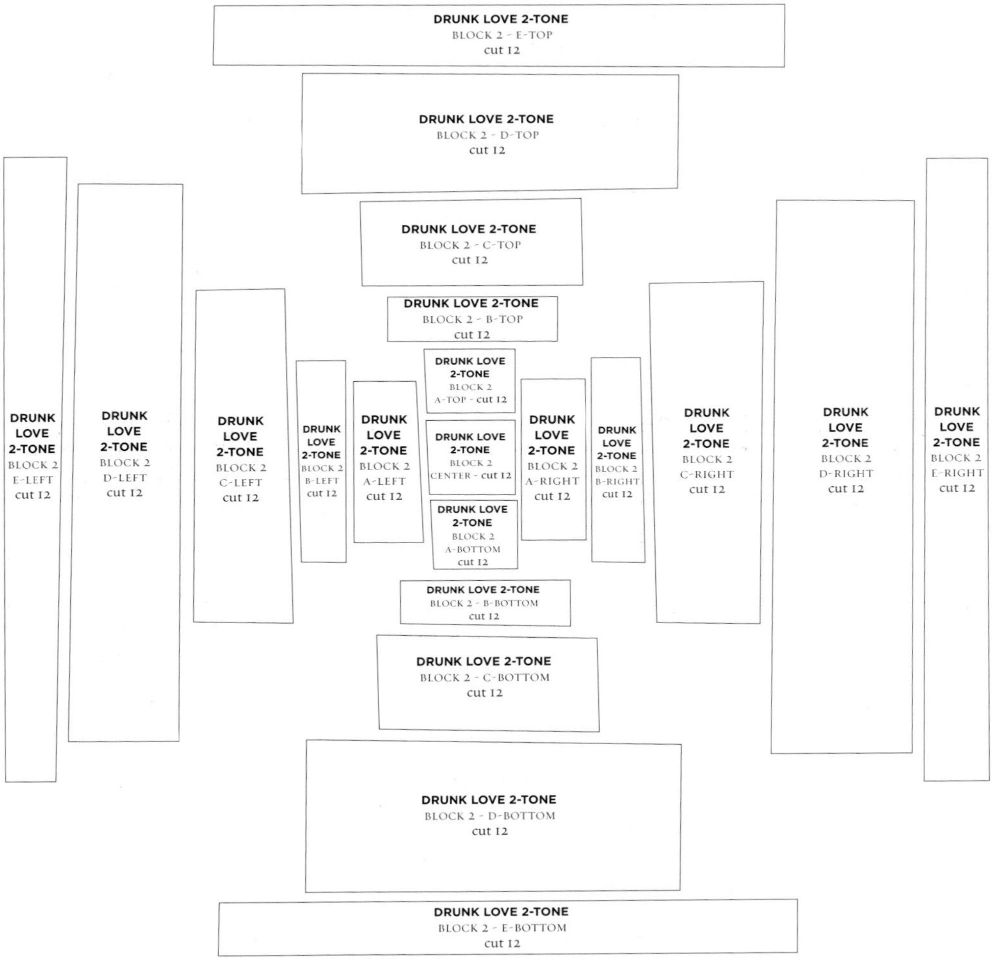

DRUNK LOVE 2-TONE BLOCK 2 - E-TOP cut 12
DRUNK LOVE 2-TONE BLOCK 2 - D-TOP cut 12
DRUNK LOVE 2-TONE BLOCK 2 - C-TOP cut 12
DRUNK LOVE 2-TONE BLOCK 2 - B-TOP cut 12
DRUNK LOVE 2-TONE BLOCK 2 A-TOP - cut 12
DRUNK LOVE 2-TONE BLOCK 2 CENTER - cut 12
DRUNK LOVE 2-TONE BLOCK 2 A-BOTTOM cut 12
DRUNK LOVE 2-TONE BLOCK 2 E-LEFT cut 12
DRUNK LOVE 2-TONE BLOCK 2 D-LEFT cut 12
DRUNK LOVE 2-TONE BLOCK 2 C-LEFT cut 12
DRUNK LOVE 2-TONE BLOCK 2 B-LEFT cut 12
DRUNK LOVE 2-TONE BLOCK 2 A-LEFT cut 12
DRUNK LOVE 2-TONE BLOCK 2 A-RIGHT cut 12
DRUNK LOVE 2-TONE BLOCK 2 B-RIGHT cut 12
DRUNK LOVE 2-TONE BLOCK 2 C-RIGHT cut 12
DRUNK LOVE 2-TONE BLOCK 2 D-RIGHT cut 12
DRUNK LOVE 2-TONE BLOCK 2 E-RIGHT cut 12
DRUNK LOVE 2-TONE BLOCK 2 - B-BOTTOM cut 12
DRUNK LOVE 2-TONE BLOCK 2 - C-BOTTOM cut 12
DRUNK LOVE 2-TONE BLOCK 2 - D-BOTTOM cut 12
DRUNK LOVE 2-TONE BLOCK 2 - E-BOTTOM cut 12

(CONTINUED)

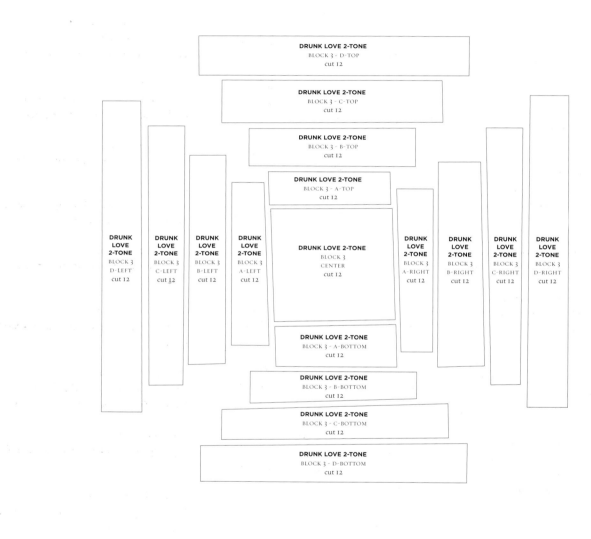

DRUNK LOVE 2-TONE
BLOCK 3 - D-TOP
cut 12

DRUNK LOVE 2-TONE
BLOCK 3 - C-TOP
cut 12

DRUNK LOVE 2-TONE
BLOCK 3 - B-TOP
cut 12

DRUNK LOVE 2-TONE
BLOCK 3 - A-TOP
cut 12

DRUNK LOVE 2-TONE
BLOCK 3
CENTER
cut 12

DRUNK LOVE 2-TONE
BLOCK 3 - A-BOTTOM
cut 12

DRUNK LOVE 2-TONE
BLOCK 3 - B-BOTTOM
cut 12

DRUNK LOVE 2-TONE
BLOCK 3 - C-BOTTOM
cut 12

DRUNK LOVE 2-TONE
BLOCK 3 - D-BOTTOM
cut 12

DRUNK LOVE 2-TONE
BLOCK 3
D-LEFT
cut 12

DRUNK LOVE 2-TONE
BLOCK 3
C-LEFT
cut 12

DRUNK LOVE 2-TONE
BLOCK 3
B-LEFT
cut 12

DRUNK LOVE 2-TONE
BLOCK 3
A-LEFT
cut 12

DRUNK LOVE 2-TONE
BLOCK 3
A-RIGHT
cut 12

DRUNK LOVE 2-TONE
BLOCK 3
B-RIGHT
cut 12

DRUNK LOVE 2-TONE
BLOCK 3
C-RIGHT
cut 12

DRUNK LOVE 2-TONE
BLOCK 3
D-RIGHT
cut 12

RESOURCES

QUILTING SERVICES

Little Red Quilt House (machine-quilting)
20 Wilson Street
Fairfield, CT 06825
203-258-9464
www.lrqh.com

Quilting Plus (Amish hand-quilting)
225 5th Avenue SW
Rochester, MN 55902
507-289-3892
quiltingplus55902@yahoo.com

QUILTING BOOKS

Dietrich, Mimi, and Roxi Eppler. *The Easy Art of Appliqué: Techniques for Hand, Machine and Fusible Appliqué.* Woodinville, WA: That Patchwork Place, 1994.

Noble, Maurine. *Machine Quilting Made Easy.* Woodinville, WA: That Patchwork Place, 1994.

Pahl, Ellen, ed. *The Quilter's Ultimate Visual Guide: From A to Z—Hundreds of Tips and Techniques for Successful Quiltmaking.* Emmaus, PA: Rodale Press, 1998.

Pellman, Rachel T. *Tips for Quilters: A Handbook of Hints, Shortcuts and Practical Suggestions from Experienced Quilters.* Intercourse, PA: Good Books, 1993.

Townswick, Jane, and Suzanne Nelson, ed. *Quiltmaking Tips & Techniques: Over 1,000 Creative Ideas to Make Your Quiltmaking Quicker, Easier, and a Lot More Fun.* Emmaus, PA: Rodale Press, 1997.

DESIGN/COLOR/INSPIRATION BOOKS

Arnett, William, ed. *The Quilts of Gee's Bend.* Atlanta: Tinwood Books, 2002.

Atkins, Jacqueline M., and Phyllis A. Tepper. *New York Beauties: Quilts from the Empire State.* New York: Dutton Studio Books, 1992.

Crow, Nancy. *Improvisational Quilts.* Concord, CA: C&T Publishing, 1995.

Holstein, Jonathan. *Abstract Design in American Quilts: A Biography of an Exhibition.* Louisville, KY: The Kentucky Quilt Project, 1991.

Horton, Roberta. *Plaids and Stripes: The Use of Directional Fabric in Quilts.* Concord, CA: C&T Publishing, 1997.

Itten, Johannes. *The Elements of Color.* New York: Wiley, 1970.

Penders, Mary Coyne. *Color and Cloth.* New York: McGraw-Hill/Contemporary Books, 1988.

Safford, Carleton L., and Robert Bishop. *America's Quilts and Coverlets.* New York: Weathervane Books, 1974.

Wahlman, Maude Southwell. *Signs and Symbols: African Images in African-American Quilts.* New York: Studio Books, 1993.

Watts, Katherine, with Elizabeth Walker. *Anna Williams: Her Quilts and Their Influences.* Paducah, KY: American Quilter's Society, 1995.

MAGAZINES

Quilter's Newsletter
www.quiltersnewsletter.com

Surface Design Journal
www.surfacedesign.org

QUILT AND CRAFT WEBSITES

www.churchofcraft.org
How-to, tips, and community events

www.craftpop.com
Guide to popular homemade arts, crafts, hobbies, ideas, and other DIY resources

www.craftster.org
Where crafty hipsters share clever ideas

www.getcrafty.com
Forums, blogs, and articles by and for crafty women around the world

www.makeworkshop.com
School, design studio, forum, and retail showroom

www.nancycrow.com
Artwork and classes by Ohio quiltmaker Nancy Crow

www.quiltalliance.org
Nonprofit organization that focuses on quilts as both works of art and pieces of history

www.quilterscache.com
Quilting instructions and hundreds of free patterns

www.quilthistory.com
Forum for people interested in antique quilts and related textiles

www.quiltindex.org
Research and reference tool on American quilts and quilt making

www.quiltstudy.org
The International Quilt Study Center at the University of Nebraska, Lincoln

www.womenfolk.com
Quilting history

CRAFTY BLOGS

www.avenueb.org/hiptopiecesquares
"A modern gal's views on quilting & fabric"

www.dioramarama.com/kmel/
"Sewing, knitting, embroidery, decorating, gardening, and other things traditionally associated with housewifery"

www.megan.scatterbrain.org/notmartha
"Daily finds and stuff I really like"

www.sewwrong.com
"Mama didn't raise a seamstress"

QUILT AND SEWING SUPPLIES/FABRIC

Hancock's of Paducah
www.hancocks-paducah.com
800-845-8723

Handloom Batik
www.handloombatik.com
212-925-9542

Keepsake Quilting
www.keepsakequilting.com
800-525-8086

Omnigrid™ Rulers, Omnigrid® Cutting Tools, and Collins Quiltmaking Notions courtesy of Prym-Dritz Corporation
PO Box 5028
Spartanburg, SC 29304
www.dritz.com

KIMONO FABRIC

kyotokimono.com
ichiroya.com
Katiesvintagekimono.com

MISCELLANEOUS SUPPLIES

Atlantic Spice Company
(sachet and eye pillow fill)
www.atlanticspice.com
800-316-7965

San Francisco Herb Company
(sachet and eye pillow fill)
www.sfherb.com
800-227-4530

ASSOCIATIONS/PLACES OF INTEREST

American Craft Council
www.craftcouncil.org
212-274-0630

American Quilter's Society
www.americanquilter.com
800-626-5420

American Textile History Museum
www.athm.org
978-441-0400

Haystack Mountain School of Crafts
www.haystack-mtn.org
207-348-2306

Quilt San Diego/Quilt Visions
www.quiltvisions.org
858-484-5201

The Textile Museum
www.textilemuseum.org
202-667-0441

INDEX

DEDICATION

This book is dedicated to my parents, Claire and Alexander Schmidt.

———————

ACKNOWLEDGMENTS

Thanks to everyone at Chronicle, especially Leigh Anna McFadden and Mikyla Bruder, for making this project happen in the first place and for their unflagging support and encouragement. Also thanks to Bethany Lyttle and Susie Cushner and her talented team, for their enthusiasm, dedication, and great work. Special thanks to Eileen O'Connor for helping me find my voice and sense of humor in the text (and in life); Richard Killeaney for everything; Alison Haney for her beautiful and capable hands; Frank Poole for photo guidance; Denese Carbonell, whose even-cuter cats inspired my Steve; and Jo-anne Usher, Megan Killeaney, and Barbara Bergantz for help with projects. Thanks to all the amazing and talented people who have worked with me over the years. Last and most definitely not least: I couldn't have done this project (or much else) without the support, inspiration, and love of my family and friends—thanks to all of you.